95 World Bank Discussion Papers

Education and Development

Evidence for New Priorities

Wadi D. Haddad,
Martin Carnoy,
Rosemary Rinaldi, and
Omporn Regel

The World Bank
Washington, D.C.

Copyright © 1990
The International Bank for Reconstruction
and Development/THE WORLD BANK
1818 H Street, N.W.
Washington, D.C. 20433, U.S.A.

All rights reserved
Manufactured in the United States of America
First printing August 1990

Discussion Papers present results of country analysis or research that is circulated to encourage discussion and comment within the development community. To present these results with the least possible delay, the typescript of this paper has not been prepared in accordance with the procedures appropriate to formal printed texts, and the World Bank accepts no responsibility for errors.

The findings, interpretations, and conclusions expressed in this paper are entirely those of the author(s) and should not be attributed in any manner to the World Bank, to its affiliated organizations, or to members of its Board of Executive Directors or the countries they represent. The World Bank does not guarantee the accuracy of the data included in this publication and accepts no responsibility whatsoever for any consequence of their use. Any maps that accompany the text have been prepared solely for the convenience of readers; the designations and presentation of material in them do not imply the expression of any opinion whatsoever on the part of the World Bank, its affiliates, or its Board or member countries concerning the legal status of any country, territory, city, or area or of the authorities thereof or concerning the delimitation of its boundaries or its national affiliation.

The material in this publication is copyrighted. Requests for permission to reproduce portions of it should be sent to Director, Publications Department, at the address shown in the copyright notice above. The World Bank encourages dissemination of its work and will normally give permission promptly and, when the reproduction is for noncommercial purposes, without asking a fee. Permission to photocopy portions for classroom use is not required, though notification of such use having been made will be appreciated.

The complete backlist of publications from the World Bank is shown in the annual *Index of Publications,* which contains an alphabetical title list (with full ordering information) and indexes of subjects, authors, and countries and regions. The latest edition is available free of charge from the Publications Sales Unit, Department F, The World Bank, 1818 H Street, N.W., Washington, D.C. 20433, U.S.A., or from Publications, The World Bank, 66, avenue d'Iéna, 75116 Paris, France.

ISSN: 0259-210X

Wadi D. Haddad is senior education adviser, Rosemary Rinaldi an operations analyst, and Omporn Regel a research analyst in the World Bank's Population and Human Resources Department, to which Martin Carnoy is a consultant.

Library of Congress Cataloging-in-Publication Data

```
Education and development : evidence for new priorities / Wadi D.
   Haddad ... [et al.].
      p.   cm. -- (World Bank discussion papers ; 95)
   Includes bibliographical references.
   ISBN 0-8213-1624-9
   1. Education--Economic aspects.   I. Haddad, Wadi.  II. Series.
LC65.E314   1990
338.4'737--dc20                                          90-41324
                                                             CIP
```

Table of Contents

Introduction 1

The Contribution of Education to Economic and Social Development 3

    Education and Economic Growth 3
    Education and Productivity 4
    Benefit-Cost Analysis 5
    The Education of Women 10
    Education and Poverty 15

Trends in Educational Development 19

    Trends in Educational Enrollments 19
    The Educational Spending Crisis 33

Lessons from World Bank and Other Donor Experience in Education and Training 37

    Total Education Sector Lending by Multilateral and Bilateral Agencies 37
    History of Bank Investments in Education and Training 37
    Education and Training Department/Division Reviews:
    Reviews of Education and Training Operations 41
    Education and Training Department/Division Reviews:
        Reviews of Sectoral Performance 42
    Operations Evaluation Department Reviews:
        Reviews of Project Performance 42
    Operations Evaluation Department Reviews:
        Reviews of Sectoral Performance 42
    Education Sector Performance Review by Other Donor Agencies 42

Policy Issues and Directions 45

    Vocational and Academic Secondary Education 45
    The Quality and Efficiency of Education 49
    Technology in Education 56
    Sector Management 56
    Science Education 58
    Higher Education, Scientific Research and Development,
        and Technology Transfer 58
    Educational Finance Reform 60

Conclusion 67

    Where More Work is Needed 67
    Education and the Changing International Division of Labor 67
    The Knowledge Gap... 68
    Nations Face a Variety of Educational Problems
        Demanding Different Strategies 69

Bibliography 73

Tables

1	Education and Productivity: Empirical Studies in Selected Countries	5
2	Rates of Return to Males' Education	7
3	Rates of Return to Males' Education, by Level of Development	10
4	Male-Female Enrollment Ratio Gap, by Income Level and by Level of Education	11
5	Educational Participation and Women's Achievement: Selected Empirical Studies in Developing Countries	13
6	Gender Comparisons: Male-Female Labor Force Participation and Adult Literacy	13
7	Rates of Return to Education by Gender	14
8	Education, Mortality, Nutrition and Fertility: Selected Empirical Studies in Developing Countries	16
9	Total Enrollment and Growth, 1960-1984	21
10	Out-of-School 6 to 11-Year-Olds in Low-Income and Lower-Middle Income Countries	25
11	Retention Rates by Income Level	26
12	Public Recurrent Expenditures on Education as a Percentage of GNP	27
13	Public Expenditures on Education as a Percentage of Total Government Expenditures	28
14	Public Recurrent Expenditures on Education per Pupil	29
15	Public Recurrent Expenditures on Education per Pupil as a Percentage of GNP Per Capita	32
16	Comparative Flow of Education Aid, 1980-1986	38
17	Distribution of Lending for Education and Training by Region	38
18	Distribution of Investments by Type of Curricula and Level of Education	39
19	Patterns of Education Project Expenditures	39
20	Education Subsector Reviews	39
21	Reviews of Bank Experience in the Education Sector	40
22	OED Project Completion/Audit Reports in the Education Sector	41
23	Evaluation Reports on Education and Training Activities Available from Other Agencies	43
24	Vocational-Technical Education and Training Versus Academic Education: Selected Empirical Studies in Developing Countries	46
25	Improving the Quality of Education: Selected Empirical Studies in Developing Countries	51
26	Education and Technology: Selected Empirical Studies in Developing Countries	53
27	Improving Sector Management: Selected Empirical Studies in Developing Countries	56
28	Scientific and Technical Personnel by Level of Development	62

| 29 | Share of Cumulative Public Educational Expenditure Appropriated by Various Socioeconomic Groups, 1980 | 64 |
| 30 | Alternative Financing Approaches: Selected Empirical Studies of Cost Recovery and Private Education in Developing Countries | 65 |

Figures

1	Females as a Percentage of Total Enrollment, 1984	12
2	Total Enrollment, 1960-1984	20
3a	Primary School Enrollment Rates, 1960-1985	24
3b	Secondary School Enrollment Rates, 1960-1985	24
4	Retention Rates by Income Level	25

This report was prepared by Wadi D. Haddad, Senior Education Advisor, PHR and Martin Carnoy (Consultant) with Rosemary Rinaldi and Omporn Regel. The authors were assisted by an advisory group comprised of Aklilu Habte, Jacques Hallak, Ralph Harbison, Barbara Searle and Adriaan Verspoor.

1

Introduction

1.1   Education has been recognized as a cornerstone of economic and social development. More recently, however, it has become even more important to the development process as accelerated technological change and new organizations of production transform the world economy. Information, biological enhancement, and new materials -- more than machines or labor alone -- are the bases of new sources of wealth. Development in all its forms -- economic, social, and cultural -- will depend increasingly on knowledge-intensive industries, agriculture, and services. Education is a key to developing that knowledge and the sense of personal efficacy needed to adjust to rapid change.

1.2   Although these new conditions place new demands on the educational system worldwide, the continuing economic crisis has jeopardized the ability of many countries even to maintain the present levels and quality of their educational services. The "knowledge gap" -- the disparity in the capability of countries or groups within countries to participate in the gains of technological innovations and new production processes -- is growing. Many countries are falling farther behind in providing the education and training needed by their youth to create and adapt available knowledge to their environment. A widening gap has serious implications for the future economic development of those countries falling behind. It guarantees that they will be increasingly hindered in efforts to enhance and shape their own economic and social development process. Their already low standard of living could also fall.

1.3   These new conditions suggest a new message. There is a need for more and better education in all countries -- industrialized and less-industrialized, high-income and low-income. Providing universal primary schooling in India or reducing high school dropouts in the United States is each a crucial development issue in that particular society. Developing the cadre of scientific and technical personnel to lead the country into an age of transformation in information, biological, and materials sciences is important in France and Zimbabwe. But the rapid changes in the world economy and the growing gap between rich nations and poor also suggest that not all countries face the same educational problems. All countries should be striving to increase student learning and to equalize access to knowledge, and all can learn from each other in using educational techniques that work. But lower-income countries with high rates of illiteracy and children out of school may also require qualitatively different approaches to improving and expanding schools than those possible in higher-income countries with much higher average schooling levels and more resources.

1.4   Detailed data on the major areas of educational policy and practices are available to produce a new analysis of these challenges and to recommend coherent, practical policies for the future. The World Bank has been active in this field for 25 years, other international agencies such as UNESCO have collected massive amounts of data, many countries have been investigating their own education at a national and comparative level, and individual scholars worldwide have also produced a wealth of educational research. Three decades of educational analysis and investment -- much of it by the Bank -- provide a solid base for understanding the relationship between education and economic development, for analyzing the contribution of various levels and types of education, for evaluating measures to improve the quality of education, for assessing the successes and failures of past educational policies, and for suggesting concrete alternatives for countries facing different economic and educational conditions, to cope with the changed circumstances of the 1990s.

1.5   The World Bank plays a singularly important role in international lending for education. In many countries the Bank is the major source of educational advice, and other agencies increasingly follow the Bank's lead in such policy and lending. Therefore, its experiences carry particularly significant weight in how educational development and lending proceeds worldwide. An analysis of these experiences, past educational policies, and new directions for policy would make an important impact on educational change -- hence economic development -- in the coming decade.

1.6   This is therefore a particularly opportune moment for taking a fresh look at educational development and donor educational policy.

1.7   In order to address these themes on education, an extensive bibliographical review was carried out and available statistics, research results, and policy studies were scanned. Not only has there been an enormous body of statistics compiled by UNESCO and other agencies over the past 25 years on enrollment growth and educational spending and costs, but the World Bank and other international and bilateral lenders have amply documented and analyzed their vast experience in financing educational projects. In addition, these same lenders and academics have carried out hundreds of research studies on various aspects of educational policy. For presentation purposes, these available statistics and studies are divided into four sections: (1) The Contribution of Education to Economic and Social Development; (2) Trends in Educational Development; (3) Lessons from World Bank and Other Donor Experience in Assisting Education; and (4) Policy Issues and Directions. Data availability in each of these categories is assessed below. An extensive bibliography is also attached (pages 73-99).

2

The Contribution of Education to Economic and Social Development

2.1   There is now a persuasive body of theoretical and empirical evidence that investment in the formal education and training of the labor force plays a crucial role in economic development. The empirical evidence takes five main forms: (1) Growth accounting studies, which estimate the contribution to economic growth in a given time period of investment in the education of the labor force. (2) Productivity studies, which estimate the contribution of additional education to the physical productivity of workers and farmers. (3) Benefit-cost studies, which evaluate the economic contribution of formal eduction and training in terms of their private costs (earnings foregone and other expenses incurred by students while in school) and public costs, and the additional income earned by those who take the education and training. (4) Studies which estimate womens' educations' effect on long-term economic development and quality of life. (5) Studies that estimate the role of education in poverty alleviation.

2.2   The results of these studies suggest that in both developed and developing countries, educational investment has been one of the most important factors contributing to economic growth; that expenditures on education contribute positively to labor productivity; that the economic payoff to spending on education -- from both a private and public standpoint -- is high, in absolute terms and compared to other investments; and that increased education of parents -- especially mothers -- has an important impact on child health and reduced fertility at all levels of economic development.

Education and Economic Growth

2.3   Some of the earliest research on the relationship between education and economic development focused on the contribution of education to economic growth (Schultz, 1961; Denison, 1962; 1967). These attempted to account for the unexplained "residual" growth left when only changes in labor (hours worked per year) and physical capital were included in the production function (Solow, 1957). Denison found that between 1930 and 1960, 23 percent of the increase in the United States' output was due to the increased education of its labor force. Further growth accounting estimates for the United States and Europe in 1950-1962 showed a wide variation for education's contribution, from a low 2 percent in Germany to highs of 12 percent in the United Kingdom, 14 percent in Belgium, 15 percent in the United States, and 25 percent in Canada. Similar estimates for developing countries also suggest a wide variation of educational contribution, from lows of 1 to 3 percent in Mexico, Brazil, and Venezuela to 16 percent in Argentina. Other estimates for Ghana, Kenya, Nigeria, Malaysia, and the Republic of Korea, based on Schultz's method, show an education contribution in the 12 to 23 percent range (see Psacharopoulos and Woodhall, 1985, Table 2-1).

2.4   Growth accounting does not provide a criterion for educational investment policy, since it only shows that should economic growth occur simultaneously with a considerable investment in education, educational investment will account for a significant percentage of that growth. But these studies do suggest, for all their limitations, that a number of countries have achieved high economic growth with large investments in education. Furthermore, other studies, discussed below, imply that unless the indirect effects of education -- such as those on health and fertility -- are accounted for, the total impact of education on growth may be underestimated.

Education and Productivity

2.5 The single best measure of education or training's economic impact is the additional productivity of workers and farmers with more education and training over those with less. Productivity measures avoid the pitfalls associated with using earnings as a proxy for economic contribution, particularly in labor markets that are highly non-competitive, marked by barriers to entry and other distortions. But productivity comparisons are hard to come by (Metcalf, 1985) and estimating the relationship between education and productivity is beset by limitations -- individuals with different amounts of education are generally in different types of jobs, producing different products.

2.6 Nevertheless, there is evidence that education results in higher output (see Table 1, page 5). A survey for the World Bank of eighteen studies which measure the relationship in low-income countries between farmers' education and their agricultural efficiency (as measured by crop production) concluded that if a farmer had completed four years of elementary education, his productivity was, on the average, 8.7 percent higher than that of a farmer with no education (Lockheed, Jamison and Lau, 1980). This is an average of results from 31 data sets, which yield both negative and highly positive education effects (a standard deviation of 9 percent). The survey also found that the effect of education is higher where complementary inputs are available. Further evidence on the effect of education in raising farmers' productivity appears in World Bank studies carried out in the Republic of Korea, Malaysia and Thailand (Jamison and Lau, 1982), and more recently in Nepal and again in Thailand (Jamison and Moock, 1984). Other studies (for example, Sack, Carnoy, and Lecaros, 1980), although reporting mixed results, support the general conclusion that education contributes positively to agricultural productivity, especially where other inputs are available to farmers and land reform has created favorable conditions for a range of production choices.

2.7 A few attempts have also been made to analyze the effect of education on productivity in industry (for a review, see Berry, 1980; also see Fuller, 1970; Min, 1987). Berry's review suggests that there is little conclusive evidence that education has a positive effect on productivity in urban areas. Fuller's research in two electrical machinery factories in Bangalore, India shows that there is a positive effect of education and training on output, especially when that training is in-firm. Min's study of academically and vocationally-educated workers in a Chinese automobile factory also shows a small, but statistically significant, increase in productivity associated with more education, and a 6 to 11 percent higher productivity for those with vocational schooling than for those with academic schooling.

2.8 The main reason that it is so difficult to get significant results in urban areas is that such studies (and those in agriculture as well [see Sack, Carnoy, and Lecaros, 1980]) is that they necessarily measure productivity-education relations in a single occupation. But the main payoff to additional education is the opportunity to move into higher-paying occupations. Workers with higher than average levels of education in a given occupation are not representative of all workers within that level, since more motivated workers with these higher levels of education have moved into higher paying jobs. Thus, such studies tend to underestimate the payoff to more education. In that sense, wage differences may provide a more accurate picture

Table 1. Education and Productivity: Empirical Studies in Selected Countries

Study	Data Base	Results
Patrick and Kehrberg (1973)	Five agricultural regions in Brazil in 1969, individual farmers	Education has a positive and significant effect. Value added in agriculture in modernizing areas, but not in traditional and already modern areas.
Pachico and Ashby (1976)	Four agricultural regions in Brazil in 1970, individual farmers	Additional productivity associated with more education much higher in the two modernizing zones, where additional, non-educational inputs are available.
Lockheed, Jamison, and Lau (1980)	Survey of 18 studies, meta-analysis	A farmer with 4 years of education had an average productivity 8.7 percent higher than one with no education. With complementary inputs, return was higher (13 percent).
Jamison and Lau (1982)	Survey data on types of farms, education of farmer, physical inputs, and outputs in Korea, Malaysia, and Thailand	Effect of education on output is positive, significant, and quantitatively important.
Jamison and Moock (1984)	Data on prices of farm inputs and outputs in Thailand	No significant effect of education on prices farmers receive for output or or paid for inputs.
Jamison and Moock (1984)	Survey of 683 rural households in 2 of Nepal's 75 districts.	Significant effect of education on farmer efficiency only in wheat production. Ability and family background controlled for.
Fuller (1970)	Survey of workers in two electrical machinery factories in Bangalore, India, 1970	In-plant vocational training yields higher productivity increases than institutional vocational education.
Berry (1980)	Survey of productivity studies on urban workers	Results of such studies are inconclusive.
Min (1987)	Survey of workers in Beijing, China auto factory	Workers with vocational education have 7 percent higher productivity than workers with academic education. More years of education not significant.

of the returns to education, although productivity studies may still be useful to measure the payoff to vocational versus academic education.

Benefit-Cost Analysis

2.9   We now have benefit-cost and rate of return analyses for a large number of countries, and at different points in time (Psacharopoulos, 1985). They suggest that the economic payoff to education is high and remains high with economic growth even as educational systems expand (see Table 2 and Table 3, pages 7 and 10).

2.10 The economic appraisal of investment projects by the World Bank and other development agencies is based on calculations of the net present value of projects and also on calculations of the rate of return. The argument for the applicability of these calculations to education and how rates of return to education are estimated has been made in a number of places (for example, Blaug, 1970; Thias and Carnoy, 1972; Psacharopoulos and Woodhall, 1985). The general consensus is that although there are a number of problems with many of the empirical estimates of rates of return -- particularly in the way costs of education are measured, the fact that the samples used for the estimates are usually drawn only from the urban labor force, and that the rates of return are uncorrected for ability differences, social class differences, and unemployment differences among those with different amounts of education -- the rates still give us important insights into the relative economic payoff to education and different levels of education in different countries at different levels of development. More recent estimates of rates of return to education at different points in time in the same country (Carnoy and Marenbach, 1975; Psacharopoulos and Woodhall, 1985; Carnoy, Daley, and Hinojosa, 1988; Ryoo, 1988) give us additional insights into the changing payoffs to educational investment as countries expand their economies and educational systems.

2.11 In Table 2, rate of return estimates are shown for a large number of developed and developing countries. Where more than one estimate has been made for the same country, each estimate is shown separately, by year. The countries have been divided by level of economic development [as measured (approximately) by a number of criteria (gross domestic product per capita; absolute GDP; percent of GDP in manufacturing; percent manufactured exports; percent high-tech manufactured exports; percent females in the labor force)] into five groups: (a) industrialized, high-income economies; (b) newly-industrialized, developing economies (NICs), involved in high-tech manufacturing and sophisticated industrial exports plus high-income oil exporters; (c) middle-income, industrializing developing countries which are or are about to participate in the world high-tech production system (although India is a low-income country, it is included in this category because of the very size of its industrial base); (d) marginally industrialized, middle-income countries that are not presently or barely involved in the changes taking place in the world economy; and (e) primarily agricultural, lower-income countries.

2.12 These categories are somewhat arbitrary and most of the rates were estimated in the 1970s, when some countries were at much lower levels of development. But the division suggests: (1) that the highest overall social rates of return to education (in urban areas) are generally in the lower income, agricultural economies and in the marginally industrialized economies; (2) that the highest payoff to education in these lower-income and middle-income countries is at the primary level; and (3) that as countries industrialize, increase their GDP per capita, and invest more in education, rates of return to education tend to fall overall, and the payoff to lower education levels tends to fall relative to the payoff to higher education levels.

2.13 Furthermore, the gap between private rates of return to education and the social rates is highest in the lower and marginally industrialized middle-income countries (see Table 3). Given the high costs of higher education, the gap is particularly striking at the higher education level. But there also appears to be a large private-social rate gap at the secondary level in marginally-industrialized, middle-income countries. This has implications for alternatives to financing education, especially in low-income and middle-income countries, where new resources for financing education have become scarce as growth rates declined in the 1980s.

2.14 Great care must be taken in making such comparisons, especially given the variation in sampling and cost estimate accuracy among these reported rates. Yet, recent studies of rates

Table 2. Rates of Return to Males' Education

Country	Year	Primary	Secondary	Higher	Primary	Secondary	Higher
			Social Rate			Private Rate	
Group A							
Group A Mean [a]		26	17	12	40	20	32
Burkina Faso	1970	26	61				
	1975	28	30	22			
	1982	20	15	21			
Ethiopia	1972	20	19	10	35	23	27
Ghana	1967	18	13	16	24	17	37
Kenya	1971	22	19	9	28	33	31
	1980		13		14		
Lesotho	1980	11	19	10	16	27	36
Liberia	1983	41	17	8	99	30	17
Malawi	1978		15				
	1982	15	15	12	16	17	47
Sierra Leone	1971	20	22	10			
Somalia	1983	21	10	20	60	13	33
Sudan	1974		8	4		13	15
Tanzania	1982		5				
Uganda	1965	66	29	12			
Group B							
Group B Mean [a]		28	17	13	46	29	26
Botswana	1983	42	41	15	99	76	38
Côte d'Ivoire	1987				26	31	25
Morocco	1970	50	10	13			
Nigeria	1966	23	13	17	30	14	34
Pakistan	1975	13	9	8	20	11	27
	1979				15	7	9
Paraguay	1982	14	11	13			
Group C							
Group C Mean [a]		28	13	13	24	15	19
Colombia	1973			18	15	15	21
	1976						25
	1981		10				
Costa Rica	1974				13	9	26
India	1965	13	16	10	17	19	16
	1978	29	14	11	33	20	13
Indonesia	1977				26	16	
	1978	22	16	15			
Peru	1972	47	20	16			
	1974	34	9	15			
	1980	41	3	16			
Philippines	1971	7	6	8	9	6	9
	1977			8			16
Thailand	1970	30	13	11	56	14	14
	1972	63	31	18			
Turkey	1968			8		24	26

Table 2 (cont.). Rates of Return to Males' Education

Country	Year	Primary	Secondary	Higher	Primary	Secondary	Higher
			Social Rate			Private Rate	
Group E							
Group E Mean [a]		16	16	12	24	18	20
Brazil	1970		24	13		25	14
Chile	1959	24	17	12			
Greece	1962		6	14		7	14
	1977	16	6	4	20	6	6
Hong Kong	1976		15	12		19	25
Israel	1958	16	7	7	27	7	8
Rep of Korea	1967		9	5			
	1969		11	10			
	1971		15	9		16	16
	1973		12	9			
	1974		17	15		21	22
	1979		11	14		13	19
	1980		8	12			
	1986		9	11		10	18
Malaysia	1978					33	34
Mexico	1963	25	17	23	32	23	39
Singapore	1966	7	18	14		20	25
Taiwan	1970		26	15		18	18
Venezuela	1984				32	12	21
Yugoslavia	1969	9	15	3	8	15	3
Group F							
Group F Mean [a]			10	10		13	12
Australia	1969					14	14
	1976			16		8	21
Austria	1981					11	4
Belgium	1960		17	7		21	9
Canada	1961		12	14		16	20
Denmark	1964			8			10
France	1962				14	12	9
	1969		10	11	16	12	10
	1976				14	11	9
Germany	1964						5
	1978					6	11
Great Britain	1971		11	7		14	27
	1972		4	8		12	10
	1973		8	8		6	16
	1975		7	7		9	22
	1977		8	6		9	17
	1978		9	7		11	23
Italy	1969					17	18
Japan	1967						10
	1973		5	6		6	8
	1976	10	9	7	13	10	9
	1980			6			8
Netherlands	1965		5	6		8	10
New Zealand	1966		19	13		20	15

Table 2 (cont.). Rates of Return to Males' Education

Country	Year	Primary	Secondary	Higher	Primary	Secondary	Higher
			Social Rate			Private Rate	
Norway	1966		7	8		7	8
Spain	1971	17	9	13	32	10	16
Sweden	1967		10	9			10
U.S.A.	1939		18	11			
	1949		14	11			
	1959		10	11			
	1969		11	11		19	15
	1969 b					14	11
	1979 b					18	10
	1982 b					24	13
	1985 b					22	14

ª The mean for each group is calculated by first estimating a mean for each country where more than one rate is available, then estimating a simple arithmetic mean.

ᵇ Rates from M. Carnoy, H. Daley, R. Hinojosa, "The Changing Economic Position of Minorities and Women in the U.S. Labor Market Since 1959," Stanford University (mimeo) -- rates are for white males only.

Sources: G. Psacharopoulos, "Returns to Education: A Further International Update and Implications." *Journal of Human Resources*, Vol. 20, No. 4 (1985), pp. 583-604; Appendix Table A-1. Côte d'Ivoire: A.G. Komenan, "Education, Experience et Salaires en Cote d'Ivoire," World Bank Discussion Paper, June, 1987; Republic of Korea, 1974, 1979, and 1986: J. Ryoo, "Changes in Rates of Return to Education: A Case Study of Korea." Unpublished Ph.D. Dissertation, Stanford University, 1988. United States.

of return over time in the United States and Korea using large census samples support the tendencies revealed by the cross-sectional data. In the United States, rates to secondary education fell relative to higher education payoffs from 1939 to 1959, stabilized in the tight labor market of the 1960s, rose relative to higher education in the early 1970s (Freeman, 1976; Psacharopoulos, 1980), but continued their secular decline in the late 1970s and 1980s (Carnoy, Daley, and Hinojosa, 1988). The Korean rates show a similar relative decline of secondary rates between 1974 and 1986 (Ryoo, 1988). Ryoo's estimates confirm the trend in other estimates for that country.

2.15   Despite the tendency for the average rate of return to education to fall with economic development, rates stay high compared to alternative investments. The main implications for policy lie in the changing structure of rates to different levels of schools as countries expand their economies and educational systems. It is not surprising that as countries industrialize and achieve universal primary education and large fractions of young people attending secondary school, the payoff to primary education falls relative to secondary and higher education. And as economies move into high levels of industrialization and universal secondary education, the payoff to that level falls relative to university. Although serious problems in the quality of primary and secondary education may continue to exist even when it is universal (in the United States, for example), the payoff to expanding access to those levels is likely lower than to expanding university. [We discuss the payoff to quality of education in more detail on page 49.] All this suggests that economies at different levels of development face very different educational investment problems and choices.

Table 3. Rates of Return to Males' Education, by Level of Development

	Level of Education					
	Primary	Secondary	Higher	Primary	Secondary	Higher
Level of Development	Social Rates			Private Rates		
Primary Product, Low-Income	26	17	12	40	20	32
Marginal Industrial, Middle-Income	28	17	13	46	29	26
Industrializing, Middle-Income, High Education	28	13	13	24	15	19
Newly-Industrialized	16	16	12	24	18	20
Industrialized	n.a.	10	10	n.a.	13	12

The Education of Women

2.16 Young women get less education than young men in almost every country. A recent World Bank study found that in the last thirty years, women in developing countries have increased their average years of schooling by about 0.6 years more than males have (Horn and Arriagada, 1986), but despite this increase, women's enrollment in primary and secondary education is lower than that of men by at least ten percentage points in 66 of 108 countries and is higher in only eight countries (Sivard, 1985). The gap is the greatest in the low-income countries and lowest in the upper-middle and high-income countries, increasing in higher levels of education (see Table 4, page 11; and Figure 1, page 12). Among areas of the world, the female-male gap is the highest in the Middle East/North Africa and the lowest in Latin America, followed by Eastern Africa.

2.17 A review of 80 empirical studies on the determinants of educational participation and achievement of women in developing countries (Stromquist, 1988) suggests that family economic conditions are more important than school-related variables (such as distance from school, adequate sanitary facilities, and the existence of a library) in explaining this gap (see also, Bowman and Anderson, in Kelly and Elliott, 1982). The poorer the household, the greater the tendency for parents to rely on daughters for domestic duties and to save educational investments for their sons. Cultural and religious factors such as early marriage and rigid rules that define women strictly as mothers and wives affect both girls' enrollment and their length of schooling (see also, Smock, 1981). This is especially true in low-income countries, in low-income regions, and in rural areas, reflecting the strongly negative interactive impact on girls education of religion and low socioeconomic class. Furthermore, the behavior of the school and the family reinforce each other, not in explicit actions but by failing to take steps to combat gender asymmetries. The school does not encourage families to send daughters to school, and the parents and communities do not pressure schools to offer suitable facilities and learning experiences for their daughters. As Stromquist points out, the state is the crucial actor for change. Without explicit government policies to promote the equal schooling of girls (including the provision of adequate facilities), it is unlikely that family practices will be changed.

Table 4. Male-Female Enrollment Ratio Gap by Income Level and by Level of Education

	Total Enrollment (M+F)					% Gap			
	1960	1970	1980	1984		1960	1970	1980	1984
Primary									
Low Income Countries	145,411	191,527	277,024	270,797	(W)	26.0	26.0	16.0	12.0
					(U)	41.4	32.0	20.6	21.8
Lower-Middle Income Countries	37,242	60,654	95,442	105,692	(W)	14.0	12.0	8.0	4.0
					(U)	18.2	15.4	10.4	4.2
Upper-Middle Income Countries	42,838	63,408	83,283	88,385	(W)	6.0	6.0	4.0	4.0
					(U)	7.8	6.8	3.6	4.4
High Income Countries	69,693	68,377	65,962	63,385	(W)	2.0	2.0	4.0	2.0
					(U)	10.8	10.8	4.6	3.2
Secondary									
Low Income Countries	26,993	51,337	98,425	99,564	(W)	56.0	44.0	24.0	22.0
					(U)	62.0	50.6	39.0	44.0
Lower-Middle Income Countries	3,950	12,000	25,747	31,915	(W)	32.0	30.0	16.0	6.0
					(U)	33.6	27.0	17.2	4.6
Upper-Middle Income Countries	8,753	20,552	26,363	35,821	(W)	16.0	12.0	6.0	6.0
					(U)	13.6	12.6	5.8	2.2
High Income Countries	28,443	49,948	54,966	57,588	(W)	4.0	4.0	0.0	2.0
					(U)	18.6	10.4	5.0	4.0
Tertiary									
Low Income Countries	2,125	3,333	7,119	8,485	(W)	60.0	68.0	56.0	48.0
					(U)	74.0	67.6	55.6	58.0
Lower-Middle Income Countries	658	1,912	4,435	6,645	(W)	30.0	26.0	16.0	26.0
					(U)	59.3	52.4	30.8	19.6
Upper-Middle Income Countries	1,233	2,905	6,373	7,691	(W)	40.0	28.0	14.0	18.0
					(U)	38.4	28.6	13.8	13.0
High Income Countries	5,883	14,079	20,768	22,115	(W)	34.0	24.0	6.0	22.0
					(U)	39.2	32.6	16.2	12.0

Note: (W) = Weighted Mean (U) = Unweighted Mean

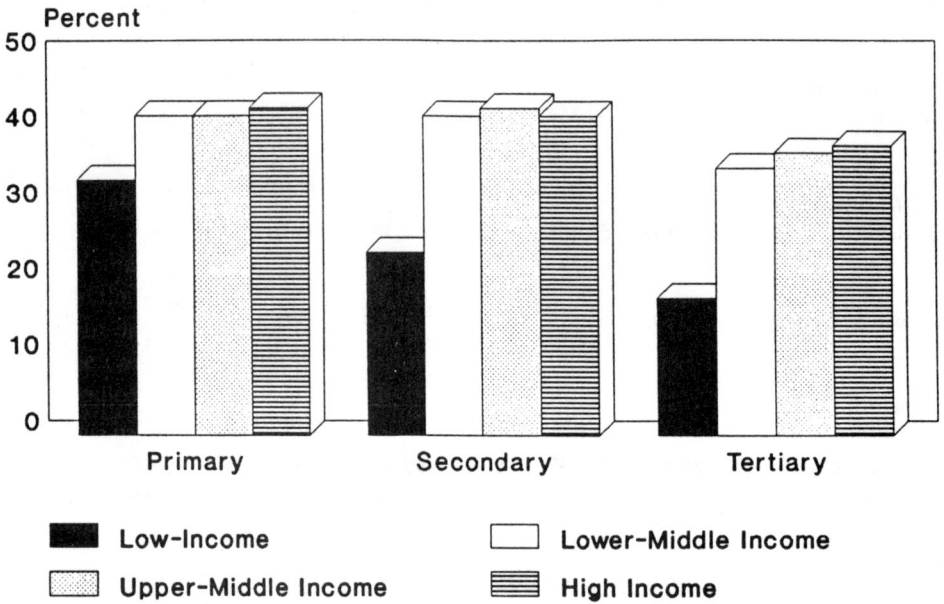

Figure 1. Females as a Percentage of Total Enrollment, 1984

2.18   Why is it important to increase female education? Besides the obvious equity argument, it is now evident from the accumulated evidence that when women receive low levels of education, it hinders economic development and reinforces social inequality (Table 5 has a review of two empirical studies on the determinants of women's educational achievement and on the role of education in women's labor force participation and income; Table 6 lists female labor force participation and adult literacy, by country in 1960 and 1980).

2.19   Women represent an enormous potential source of human capital and of scientific and technical skills in both agriculture and industry. The rate of return to investing in women's education in developing countries is as high or higher, even as measured by income differences alone (without accounting for fertility and child health effects), as men's (see Table 7; Psacharopoulos and Woodhall, 1985; Ryoo, 1988).

2.20   Women constitute an important source of skills in rapidly expanding electronic and communications manufacturing, and financial and computer services (Carnoy, 1985). It could be argued that the existence of a well-educated female labor force with industrial experience is the single most important factor governing the location of high-tech industry and services. Whereas these are highly gender-segregated industries in both developed and developing countries (Strober and Arnold, 1987; Kim, 1987), they do provide non-agricultural occupational opportunities for women and appear to contribute to changing male-female relations in the NICs (Kim, 1987). The lack of an educated female labor force could seriously hinder industrializing countries with high female illiteracy from participating in high-tech industrialization.

**Table 5. Educational Participation and Women's Achievement:
Selected Empirical Studies in Developing Countries**

Study	Data Base	Results
Stromquist (1988)	Eighty available empirical studies	Family economic conditions are important in affecting women's education, with poorer households tending to keep daughters at home. Cultural and religious factors affect both girls' enrollment and length of schooling, but religion seems neutralized as parents income and education increases.
Sivard (1985)	Review of world-wide statistics on women's labor force and educational characteristics	In most of world, increased participation of women in wage labor in 1960-80. But women's unemployment higher, wages lower than men's. Women are segregated in women's jobs. Agriculture is still principal employer of women in developing countries. Women are much poorer than men.

Table 6. Gender Comparisons: Male-Female Labor Force Participation and Adult Literacy

Region	1980 GNP per capita (US$)	Labor Force Participation						Adult Literacy					
		1960 Rate		1980 Rate		Ratio of Women's Rate to Men's (Men=100%)		1960 Rate		1980 Rate		Ratio of Women's Rate to Men's (Men=100%)	
		Wom. (%)	Men (%)	Wom. (%)	Men (%)	1960	1980	Wom. (%)	Men (%)	Wom. (%)	Men (%)	1960	1980
World	2,621	47	90	46	85	52	54	59	68	68	78	87	87
America													
North America	11,233	41	88	50	83	47	60	98	97	99	99	101	100
Latin America	2,172	21	90	25	84	23	30	63	70	81	85	90	95
Europe													
Western Europe	9,840	37	91	43	85	41	51	93	96	97	98	97	99
Eastern Europe & USSR	4,480	67	88	69	82	76	84	94	97	97	99	97	98
Asia													
Middle East	3,046	31	91	25	85	34	29	15	39	46	71	38	65
South Asia	226	39	91	36	85	43	42	13	40	31	56	32	55
Far East	1,045	57	90	53	86	63	62	60	77	81	90	78	90
Oceania	8,102	37	92	46	87	40	53	90	91	91	93	99	98
Africa	806	44	92	42	88	48	48	12	27	36	57	44	63

Source: "Women ... A World Survey." R.L. Sivard, 1985.

Table 7. Rates of Return to Education by Gender

Country	Year	Educational Level	Men	Women
Australia	1976	University	21.1	21.2
Austria	1981	All	10.3	13.5
Colombia	1973	All-urban	18.1	20.8
		-rural	10.3	20.1
Costa Rica	1974	All	14.7	14.7
France	1969	Secondary	13.9	15.9
		University	22.5	13.8
	1976	Secondary	14.8	16.2
		University	20.0	12.7
Germany	1974	All	13.1	11.2
	1977	All	13.6	11.7
Great Britain	1971	Secondary	10.0	8.0
		University	8.0	12.0
Greece	1977	All	4.7	4.5
Japan	1976	University	6.9	6.9
	1980	University	5.7	5.8
Peru [a]	1985	Primary		12.0
		Secondary, Gen.		8.0
		Secondary, Tech.		8.5
		University		15.5
South Korea	1971	Secondary	13.7	16.9
		University	15.7	22.9
	1976	All	10.3	1.7
	1980	All	17.2	5.0
Sri Lanka	1981	All	6.9	7.9
Portugal	1977	All	7.5	8.4
Puerto Rico	1959	Primary	29.5	18.4
		Secondary	27.3	40.8
		University	21.9	9.0
Taiwan	1982	Primary	8.4	16.1
Thailand	1971	All	9.1	13.0
Venezuela	1984	All	9.9	13.5

[a] E. King, "Does Education Pay in the Labor Market? Women's Labor Force Participation, Occupation, and Earnings in Peru," The World Bank, September, 1988 (mimeo).

Source: Psacharopoulos (1985) "Returns to Education: A Further International Update and Implications," *Journal of Human Resources* XX:4.

2.21 Rapid population growth has made raising the standard of living in many countries difficult. A bulging population of young people also strains education budgets and, in many low-income countries an increasing absolute number of young people get no education at all. These are the children of rural and low-income families, implying increasing disparities between urban and rural areas and between an emerging urban middle class and the poor. Reducing fertility rates is therefore an important part of any development program, and reduced fertility depends heavily on women's education (Cochrane, 1979) where, particularly in low-income (low literacy) countries, education levels for men and especially women have to reach a "threshold" in order to have a negative effect on fertility. These results are largely confirmed by cross-national studies of world fertility survey data (for example, United

Nations, 1983), except that increasing men's and women's education are equally good explainers of declining fertility rates. The analysis also shows a distinct threshold effect in low-income countries at completed primary education (see Table 8, page 16).

2.22   Women's education is closely related to child health, as measured either by nutritional status or infant and child mortality (Cochrane, O'Hara and Leslie, 1980). Although the exact mechanism through which education acts to affect child health is unclear, there is an unequivocal schooling effect which is distinct from the effect of income differences (associated with higher education) on child health (Table 8). Improved child nutrition and health, in turn, plays an important role in school achievement and attainment (Moock and Leslie, 1986). Women's education is therefore crucial to breaking the vicious circle of poverty being reproduced through poor child health and low levels of education.

Education and Poverty

2.23   From the considerable research in developed countries -- mainly the United States -- we know that in and of itself, education cannot eliminate poverty. But by developing skills that individuals can use for increasing their income (either through increased self-employed productivity or increased productivity in wage labor), by contributing to better health, and by reducing fertility, education, especially when combined with investments in other factors of production, can contribute to economic growth, to an increased percentage of the labor force with better-paying work, and the increased standard of living of a smaller family.

2.24   There has been a long debate in the United States on this issue (see, for example, Moynihan, 1967; Ribich, 1968; Thurow, 1970; Sowell, 1977; Smith and Welch, 1986; Carnoy, Daley, and Hinojosa, 1988) which -- although specific to the multiethnic nature of society in the United States -- provides insights for developing countries. In brief, U.S. data suggest that increasing education among Black and Hispanic males and females is an important explainer of their rising relative (to non-Hispanic white male) income in a historical period marked by economic growth and somewhat equalizing income distribution. In the late 1970s and 1980s, when economic growth occurred but income distribution in the labor force became significantly more unequal, rising minority education could not offset declining relative incomes. Nor did the poverty rate decrease with rising education. This implies that education is much more likely to contribute to poverty reduction when there is both economic growth and at least an unchanged income distribution, and at best, an income distribution that is becoming more equal. Therefore, to reduce poverty, the public sector has to invest in education, to plan balanced growth, and to manage an incomes policy that "lifts all boats."

2.25   It is important to add that investing in education alone will not equalize income distribution. There is considerable evidence that increasing education in the labor force contributes positively to more equal income distribution, but that the effect is small (Langoni, 1973; Chiswick and Mincer, 1972; Carnoy, et. al., 1978). Other effects, such as changes in the income distribution itself or, in the case of the United States, unemployment, are far more important. This means that the public sector cannot rely on educational investment alone to equalize income inequality, but rather needs to take other measures, such as sustainable land reform, or the implementation of progressive income-tax based government finance, to achieve this goal.

**Table 8. Education, Mortality, Nutrition and Fertility:
Selected Empirical Studies in Developing Countries**

Study	Data Base	Results
Arriaga and Davis (1969)	Secondary data on Latin American mortality rates	Prior to 1930, mortality decline was closely related to improvements in living standards rather than medical breakthroughs.
Cochrane, et.al. (1980)	Secondary data on mortality rates, by country	Literacy seems to be most important variable explaining life expectancy, even higher than number of physicians per capita. One additional year of mother's schooling results in reduction of 9 per thousand in infant mortality. Effect of husband's education about one-half of wife's.
Cochrane (1979)	Review of existing studies	Increased education tends to decrease fertility. Decrease is greater for the education of women than of men and in urban rather than rural areas. But education is likely to increase fertility in countries with the lowest level of female literacy up to completed primary schooling. In societies with higher levels of female literacy, education lowers the demand for children by altering perceived costs and benefits.
United Nations (1983)	Data from the world fertility survey of 22 developing countries	Confirms negative influence of women's (and husbands') education upon marital fertility, desired family size in 20 out of 22 countries. But levels of national development and level of family planning program efforts enhance or mitigate the strength of the education-fertility relationship. Differential fertility by education is highest in the countries with highest levels of development. The negative relationship between education and fertility is stronger in urban areas than rural. Ethnic or regional differences in the education-fertility relationship are not of primary importance.
Zachariah & Patel (1984)	Fertility decline in India, 1961-1981	Although family planning practice can account for 90% of fertility decline, family planning input variables -- manpower, budget, etc. -- were much less important than socioeconomic factors such as female education and children's health in explaining the practice of family planning.
Fertility Survey of Thailand (1977)	Individuals in Thailand	For all women married less than 20 years, education is uniformly inversely related to fertility.

Table 8 (cont.). Education, Mortality, Nutrition and Fertility: Selected Empirical Studies in Developing Countries

Study	Data Base	Results
Cravioto & Delicardi (1975)	Survey in Southwestern Mexico	No significant difference in parental education between well-nourished and malnourished children.
Christiansen, et al. (1974)	Bogota, Colombia	Significant positive association between parental education and children's nutrition.
Gans (1963)	Lagos, Nigeria	Children's weight of literate mothers was greater than illiterate mothers.
Graves (1978)	Kathmandu, Nepal	Mothers with no schooling had more malnourished children than those with schooling.
Levinson (1974)	Rural Punjab, India	Literate mothers had smaller percentage of third-degree malnourished children.

3

Trends in Educational Development

3.1   The vast amount of data available from UNESCO and national statistics on trends in educational development provide a detailed picture of the percentage of young people enrolled in primary, secondary vocational, secondary academic, and tertiary levels of education for almost every country from 1960 to 1985. They also provide data on enrollment by gender, retention rates in primary school (or, conversely, drop-out rates), educational spending (recurrent and capital) as a percentage of GNP and as a percentage of total public spending, and cost-per-student, by education level -- all by country and over time. These data are an excellent source for understanding the educational achievements and difficulties of countries at different levels of economic development.

Trends in Educational Enrollments

3.2   The data show that developing countries have expanded their educational systems rapidly over the past 25 years (see Figure 2, page 20, and Table 9, page 21). From 1960-80, the weighted (heavily influenced by the huge enrollments in China and India) average growth rate of primary enrollment in low-income countries was 3.1 percent annually, and unweighted, 7.1 percent. Secondary enrollments also increased rapidly in the low-income and lower middle-income countries, and the tertiary level grew rapidly in this period at all development levels. But, in the 1980s, the drop in enrollment growth has also been impressive, particularly at the primary and secondary level. Part of this drop is due to slower growth of the school-age population, especially in countries such as China. Yet, for many countries, the drop reflects a real slowdown in incorporating young people into schools.

3.3   The result of the slowdown is that low-income countries are still far from achieving even universal primary education (see Figures 3A and 3B, page 24, for trends in gross enrollment rates by level of development). If anything, the gap in gross enrollment rates between the lowest-income countries and the middle-income and developed countries has increased, especially since 1970 and especially at higher levels of education. This gap has become accentuated in the 1980s. Two of the most important exceptions to this trend have been India and China, which -- despite their low levels of income per capita -- have reached enrollment rates at the primary and secondary level associated with lower middle-income countries.

3.4   Because of the rapid expansion of enrollment in 1960-84, enrollment increases at the primary level per se are an issue largely in the lowest-income countries. Table 10, page 25, lists the ten developing countries with the largest populations of out-of-school children in 1985 and their projected out-of-school populations for the year 2000, based on two scenarios of enrollment growth. In 1985, 31 percent of all the world's 6 to 11-year-olds and 61 percent of all out-of-school children that age lived in these 10 countries. To reduce the number of out-of-school children, enrollment growth in these countries would have to outstrip population growth. For many low-income countries, this is a tall order. On the other hand, the fact that

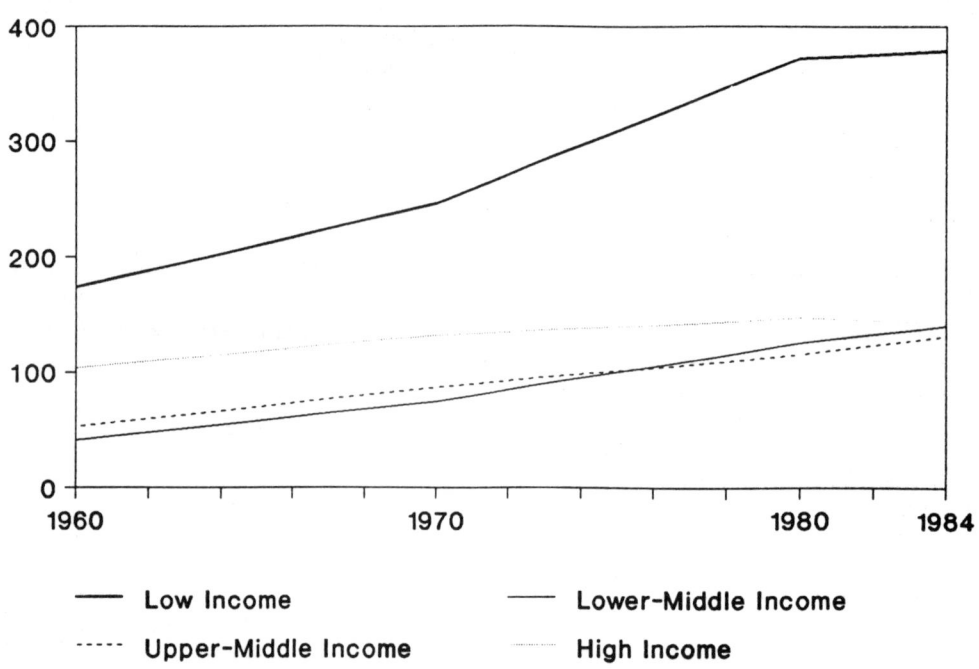

Figure 2. Total Enrollment

— Low Income
— Lower-Middle Income
----- Upper-Middle Income
.... High Income

India can reduce its out-of-school population to zero in the next 12 years if present economic growth rates are maintained, will have a significant impact on the problem at a world level.

3.5 In lower middle-income and many upper middle-income countries, the principal educational problems are retention at the primary level and an appropriate expansion of places at the secondary and higher levels (see Figure 4, page 25, and Table 11, page 26). Although retention rates vary greatly among countries at every income level (for example, the high primary retention rates in Sri Lanka and Tanzania even at low per capita income levels), retention rates can be surprisingly low even in upper middle-income countries. Yet, the tendency is to attain universal primary education and high gross enrollment rates even in secondary education as the development level rises. Attention shifts to problems of retention at the secondary level. The most important educational issues in those developing countries that are newly industrialized and that are primarily oil-producers thus revolve around improving the quality of primary, secondary and higher education rather than their expansion.

3.6 The enrollment and retention data, combined with rate of return estimates, suggest that countries at different levels of development have very different educational problems, and that appropriate policies therefore also vary substantially. In lower-income countries, the most appropriate emphasis is on delivering better quality education at the primary level and -- in many cases -- resolving the problem of high cost university (including the delivery of technical and scientific education at lower cost), and making rational choices of the most relevant type of secondary education. In higher-income countries, the emphasis has to be quite different, focusing much more on expanding and improving secondary education and producing high quality university graduates for new industries and services.

Table 9. Total Enrollment and Growth, 1960-1984

Income	Total Enrollment ('000)					Average Annual Growth Rate (%)	
	1960	1970	1980	1984		1960-1980	1980-1984

Primary

Income	1960	1970	1980	1984		1960-1980	1980-1984
Low Income Countries	145,411	191,527	277,024	270,797	(W)	3.1	0.1
					(U)	7.1	3.2
					(M)	6.6	3.0
Selected Countries with Low Enrollment							
Bhutan	3	9	30	44		12.2	10.0
Somalia	21	33	272	221		13.7	(5.1)
Selected Countries with High Enrollment							
China	93,791	105,280	146,270	135,571		2.2	(1.9)
India	34,994	57,045	73,873	81,097		3.8	2.4
Lower-Middle Income Countries	37,242	60,654	95,442	105,692	(W)	4.8	2.5
					(U)	5.3	3.0
					(M)	4.9	3.1
Selected Countries with Low Enrollment							
Botswana	36	83	172	210		8.1	5.1
Mauritania	11	32	91	107		11.1	4.1
Selected Countries with High Enrollment							
Indonesia	8,955	14,870	25,537	29,909		5.4	4.0
Nigeria	2,913	3,516	13,760	14,383		8.1	1.1
Upper-Middle Income Countries	42,838	63,408	83,283	88,385	(W)	3.4	1.5
					(U)	2.5	1.0
					(M)	2.0	0.8
Selected Countries with Low Enrollment							
Panama	162	255	338	339		3.7	0.1
Uruguay	320	354	331	350		0.2	1.4
Selected Countries with High Enrollment							
Brazil	7,458	12,812	22,598	24,789		5.7	2.3
Mexico	4,885	9,248	14,666	15,219		5.7	0.9
High-Income Countries	69,693	68,377	65,962	63,385	(W)	(0.3)	(1.0)
					(U)	1.1	0.3
					(M)	(0.2)	(0.6)
Selected Countries with Low Enrollment							
Kuwait	28	76	149	171		8.7	3.5
Trinidad & Tobago	179	226	167	168		(0.3)	0.1
Selected Countries with High Enrollment							
Japan	12,729	9,558	11,751	11,464		(0.4)	(0.6)
United States	29,965	28,700	27,448	26,839		(0.4)	(0.6)

Note: (W) = Weighted Mean (U) = Unweighted Mean (M) = Median

Table 9 (cont.). Total Enrollment and Growth, 1960-1984

Income	Total Enrollment ('000)					Average Annual Growth Rate (%)	
	1960	1970	1980	1984		1960-1980	1980-1984
Secondary							
Low Income Countries	26,993.0	51,337.0	98,425.0	99,564.0	(W)	6.7	0.3
					(U)	12.0	6.6
					(M)	11.8	6.3
Selected Countries with Low Enrollment							
Bhutan	0.0	1.0	-	6.0		-	-
Somalia	3.0	25.0	44.0	63.0		14.4	9.4
Selected Countries with High Enrollment							
China	14,778.0	26,483.0	56,778.0	48,609.0		7.0	(3.8)
India	10,125.0	20,114.0	31,597.0	37,869.0		5.9	4.6
Lower-Middle Income Countries	3,950.0	12,000.0	25,747.0	31,915.0	(W)	9.7	5.3
					(U)	11.3	6.3
					(M)	11.2	4.0
Selected Countries with Low Enrollment							
Botswana	1.0	5.0	21.0	31.0		16.4	10.2
Mauritania	1.0	4.0	22.0	-		16.7	-
Selected Countries with High Enrollment							
Indonesia	727.0	2,460.0	5,722.0	7,446.0		10.9	6.8
Nigeria	167.0	357.0	2,346.0	3,561.0		14.1	11.0
Upper-Middle Income Countries	8,753.0	20,552.0	26,363.0	35,821.0	(W)	6.5	3.1
					(U)	6.3	4.4
					(M)	5.0	2.6
Selected Countries with Low Enrollment							
Panama	39.0	78.0	171.0	182.0		7.7	1.6
Uruguay	93.0	168.0	148.0	198.0		2.4	7.5
Selected Countries with High Enrollment							
Brazil	1,177.0	4,086.0	2,819.0	2,952.0		4.5	1.2
Mexico	512.0	1,584.0	4,742.0	6,064.0		11.8	6.3
High-Income Countries	28,443.0	49,948.0	54,966.0	57,588.0	(W)	2.5	1.4
					(U)	5.4	3.5
					(M)	3.3	0.9
Selected Countries with Low Enrollment							
Kuwait	12.0	71.0	182.0	231.0		14.6	6.1
Trinidad & Tobago	24.0	53.0	89.0	92.0		6.8	0.8
Selected Countries with High Enrollment							
Japan	8,672.0	8,667.0	9,521.0	10,613.0		0.5	2.8
United States	9,600.0	19,910.0	14,556.0	13,779.0		2.1	(1.4)

Note: (W) = Weighted Mean (U) = Unweighted Mean (M) = Median

Table 9 (cont.). Total Enrollment and Growth, 1960-1984

Income	Total Enrollment ('000)					Average Annual Growth Rate (%)	
	1960	1970	1980	1984		1960-1980	1980-1984
Tertiary							
Low Income Countries	2,125.2	3,332.7	7,119.3	8,485.2	(W)	6.2	4.5
					(U)	10.2	11.7
					(M)	9.9	9.2
Selected Countries with Low Enrollment							
Bhutan	-	-	0.3	0.1		-	(24.0)
Somalia	0.1	1.0	-	-		-	-
Selected Countries with High Enrollment							
China	961.6	47.8	1,161.4	1,443.6		0.9	5.6
India	1,102.8	2,903.6	5,345.0	6,252.9		8.2	4.0
Lower-Middle Income Countries	657.6	1,911.5	4,434.8	6,645.2	(W)	9.2	8.7
					(U)	13.6	9.4
					(M)	12.7	5.4
Selected Countries with Low Enrollment							
Botswana	-	0	0.9	1.8		-	18.9
Mauritania	-	-	-	-		-	-
Selected Countries with High Enrollment							
Indonesia	-	248.2	-	980.2		-	-
Nigeria	-	15.6	150.1	181.6		-	4.9
Upper-Middle Income Countries	1,232.7	2,905.4	6,373.4	7,691.1	(W)	8.9	4.1
					(U)	8.5	5.3
					(M)	7.5	6.4
Selected Countries with Low Enrollment							
Panama	4.0	8.9	40.4	52.2		12.3	6.6
Uruguay	15.3	-	36.3	63.7		4.4	15.1
Selected Countries with High Enrollment							
Brazil	95.7	430.5	1,409.2	1,479.4		14.4	1.2
Mexico	78.6	247.6	897.7	1,071.7		12.9	4.5
High-Income Countries	5,882.6	14,079.0	20,768.4	22,114.7	(W)	6.5	1.6
					(U)	8.7	6.5
					(M)	7.4	4.1
Selected Countries with Low Enrollment							
Kuwait	-	2.7	13.6	21.9		-	12.6
Trinidad & Tobago	0.5	2.4	5.6	5.5		12.8	(0.4)
Selected Countries with High Enrollment							
Japan	789.8	1,819.3	2,412.1	2,403.4		5.7	(0.1)
United States	3,582.7	8,498.1	12,096.9	12,467.7		6.3	0.8

Note: (W) = Weighted Mean (U) = Unweighted Mean (M) = Median

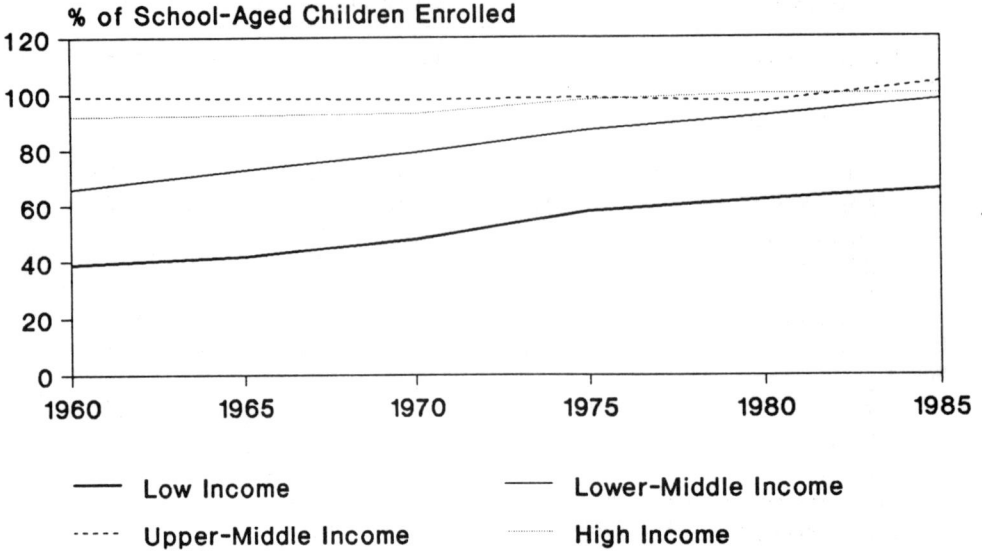

Figure 3a. Primary School Enrollment Rates, 1960-1985

Note: Figures more than 100% indicate the number of overaged students enrolled at the primary level.

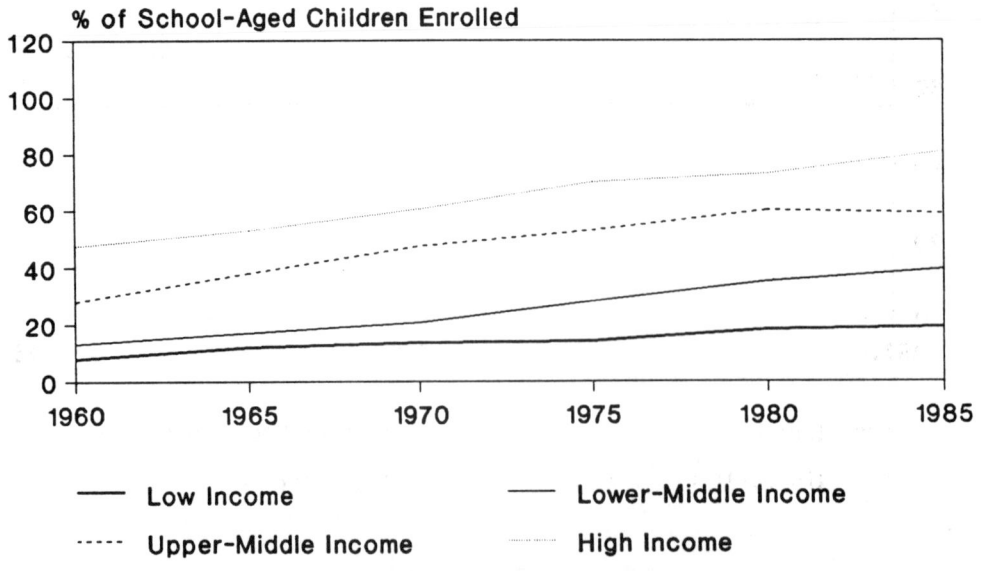

Figure 3b. Secondary School Enrollment Rates, 1960-1985

Note: Figures more than 100% indicate the number of overaged students enrolled at the primary level.

Table 10. Out-of-School 6 to 11-Year-Olds in Low-Income and Lower-Middle Income Countries
(US$ Millions)

Category	Actual 1985		Projected for 2000			
			2% Enrollment Growth		5% Enrollment Growth	
Total Out-of-School	87	(21%)	129	(25%)	52	(10%)
Selected countries:						
India	22.5	(25%)	12.6	(12%)	0.0	(0%)
Pakistan	11.0	(70%)	19.0	(76%)	13.0	(52%)
Bangladesh	6.7	(45%)	6.1	(35%)	0.0	(0%)
Ethiopia	5.5	(81%)	9.7	(87%)	7.9	(71%)
Nigeria	4.1	(26%)	14.6	(50%)	3.0	(10%)
Afghanistan	2.7	(85%)	4.8	(89%)	4.4	(81%)
Sudan	2.3	(68%)	4.4	(77%)	3.0	(53%)
Egypt	2.3	(33%)	2.8	(30%)	0.0	(0%)
Tanzania	2.0	(46%)	4.9	(64%)	2.5	(32%)
Uganda	1.4	(49%)	2.9	(60%)	1.4	(29%)

Note: Numbers in parentheses refer to out-of-school children as a percentage of the population of primary school-age children (6 to 11 years old).

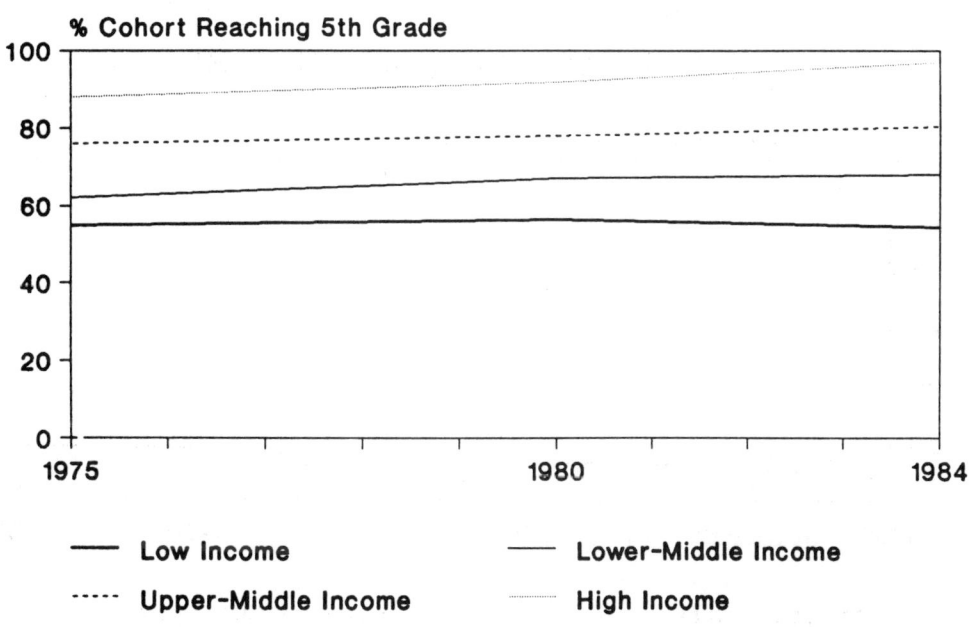

Figure 4. Retention Rates by Income Level

Table 11. Retention Rates by Income Level

		Percentage of Cohort Reaching Fifth Grade					
		Total			Female		
		1975	1980	1984	1975	1980	1984
Low Income Countries	(W)	40	44	38	37	42	41
	(U)	55	57	54	52	55	52
Selected Countries with Low Rate							
Bangladesh		-	23	23	-	23	25
Lao, People's Dem. Rep.		-	22	20	-	23	19
Selected Countries with High Rate							
Sri Lanka		65	91	95	63	91	95
Tanzania		85	84	-	81	83	-
** China		-	-	64	-	-	-
** India		37	43	-	34	38	-
Lower-Middle Income Countries	(W)	56	66	69	51	64	70
	(U)	62	68	69	63	68	69
Selected Countries with Low Rate							
Guatemala		27	32	31	28	31	28
Nicaragua		27	27	23	-	30	26
Selected Countries with High Rate							
Jordan		95	103	112	94	103	113
Mauritius		97	98	96	97	99	96
Upper-Middle Income Countries	(W)	56	60	56	81	73	72
	(U)	76	78	81	79	81	84
Selected Countries with low rate							
Brazil		32	39	38	-	-	-
Portugal		58	37	37	58	37	40
Selected Countries with High Rate							
Poland		103	99	100	-	-	-
Iraq		91	96	130	85	92	123
High Income Countries	(W)	94	99	100	95	96	101
	(U)	88	92	98	89	90	97
Selected Countries with Low Rate							
Oman		51	80	90	90	65	84
Saudi Arabia		75	78	74	78	79	71
Selected Countries with High Rate							
Singapore		105	106	103	103	107	102
United Arab Emirates		-	100	128	-	96	125

Note: (W) = Weighted Mean (U) = Unweighted Mean

Table 12. Public Recurrent Expenditures on Education as a Percentage of GNP

		1970	1975	1980	1984
Low-Income Countries	(U)	**3.0**	**3.0**	**3.3**	**2.9**
Selected Countries with Low Expenditures					
Bangladesh		-	1.1	1.5	1.8
Somalia		1.0	2.1	1.7	1.2
Selected Countries with High Expenditures					
Kenya		5.0	6.3	6.9	5.7
Tanzania		4.5	5.4	5.1	3.4
** China		1.3	1.8	2.5	2.3
** India		2.8	2.8	3.0	2.4
Lower-Middle Income Countries	(U)	**3.5**	**4.2**	**4.6**	**4.1**
Selected Countries with Low Expenditures					
Paraguay		2.2	1.6	1.6	1.6
Philippines		2.6	1.9	1.6	1.3
Selected Countries with High Expenditures					
Botswana		5.2	8.5	7.1	8.4
Congo, People's Republic		5.9	8.1	6.9	-
Upper-Middle Income Countries	(U)	**4.2**	**4.3**	**4.5**	**3.6**
Selected with Low Expenditures					
Brazil		2.9	3.0	3.4	1.0
Spain		2.1	1.8	2.3	1.9
Selected Countries with High Expenditures					
Algeria		7.8	6.7	7.8	3.5
Ireland		5.0	6.2	6.6	6.2
High-Income Countries	(U)	**5.1**	**5.6**	**5.3**	**5.1**
Selected Countries with Low Expenditures					
Hong Kong		2.6	2.7	2.5	2.8
Oman		-	1.6	2.1	3.6
Selected Countries with High Expenditures					
Canada		8.9	7.8	7.5	7.4
Sweden		7.7	7.1	9.1	8.1

Note: (U) = Unweighted Mean

Table 13. Public Expenditures on Education as a Percentage of Total Government Expenditures

		1970	1975	1980	1984
Low-Income Countries	(W)	10.6	10.3	13.2	20.0
	(U)	15.3	14.6	14.6	17.3
	(M)	17.6	15.1	11.0	16.8
Selected Countries with Low Percentage Share					
China		2.9	4.2	6.1	-
Pakistan		4.2	5.2	5.0	-
Selected Countries with High Percentage Share					
Niger		17.7	18.7	22.9	-
Rwanda		26.6	25.3	21.6	-
Lower-Middle Income Countries	(W)	18.4	14.1	9.8	19.2
	(U)	17.7	17.1	16.0	13.9
	(M)	17.1	16.4	15.2	12.5
Selected Countries with Low Percentage Share					
Syrian Arab Republic		9.4	7.8	8.1	11.2
Jamaica		11.5	9.6	11.6	10.3
Selected Countries with High Percentage Share					
Costa Rica		31.8	31.1	22.2	18.9
Ecuador		23.2	25.9	33.3	-
Upper-Middle Income Countries	(W)	11.1	10.8	14.7	2.3
	(U)	16.3	13.1	16.0	11.4
	(M)	15.2	11.9	14.9	9.8
Selected Countries with Low Percentage Share					
Hungary		6.9	4.2	5.2	6.4
Romania		8.0	6.4	6.7	-
Selected Countries with High Percentage Share					
Algeria		31.6	23.0	24.3	-
Yugoslavia		23.3	24.4	32.5	-
High Income Countries	(W)	12.1	9.8	14.4	12.3
	(U)	16.1	15.0	13.4	13.3
	(M)	15.5	14.7	14.0	13.0
Selected Countries with Low Percentage Share					
Austria		8.1	8.5	8.0	8.0
Israel		8.1	7.6	7.3	-
Selected Countries with high percentage share					
France		24.9	29.5	27.1	-
Netherlands, The		29.4	23.7	23.1	-

Note: (W) = Weighted Mean (U) = Unweighted Mean (M) = Median

Table 14. Public Recurrent Expenditures on Education per Pupil

		Expenditures (US$)			Growth (%)	
		1975	1980	1984	1975-1980	1980-1984
Primary						
Low Income Countries	(W)	24.4	24.1	20.7	(0.2)	(3.7)
	(U)	44.2	40.3	28.8	(1.8)	(8.1)
	(M)	43.5	31.5	30.0	(6.3)	(1.2)
Selected Countries with Low Expenditures						
Bangladesh		4.0	6.0	9.0	8.4	10.7
Haiti		16.0	19.0	15.0	3.5	(5.7)
Selected Countries with High Expenditures						
Central African Republic		74.0	-	44.0	-	-
Mali		-	54.0	59.0	-	2.2
** China		-	-	-	-	-
** India		23.0	23.0	-	0.0	0.0
Lower-Middle Income Countries	(W)	73.4	161.4	206.4	17.1	6.3
	(U)	95.4	127.4	140.0	6.0	2.4
	(M)	89.0	87.0	108.0	(0.5)	5.6
Selected Countries with Low Expenditures						
Bolivia		72.0	82.0	51.0	2.6	(11.2)
Dominican Republic		35.0	33.0	51.0	(1.2)	11.5
Selected Countries with High Expenditures						
Côte d'Ivoire		147.0	160.0	-	1.7	-
Turkey		-	792.0	816.0	-	0.7
Upper-Middle Income Countries	(W)	213.9	273.6	233.6	5.0	(3.9)
	(U)	299.3	334.8	340.7	2.3	0.4
	(M)	206.0	229.0	300.0	2.1	7.0
Selected Countries with Low Expenditures						
Chile		86.0	181.0	241.0	16.0	7.4
Mexico		93.0	102.0	70.0	1.9	(9.0)
Selected Countries with High Expenditures						
Iran, Islamic Republic of		288.0	659.0	315.0	18.0	(16.9)
Ireland		648.0	592.0	879.0	(1.8)	10.4
High Income Countries	(W)	2,406.6	1,248.2	1,468.6	(12.3)	4.1
	(U)	1,601.2	1,550.8	1,986.9	(0.6)	6.4
	(M)	1,099.0	1,168.0	1,445.0	1.2	5.5
Selected Countries with Low Expenditures						
Hong Kong		250.0	330.0	455.0	5.7	8.4
Israel		605.0	83.0	-	(32.8)	-
Selected Countries with High Expenditures						
Kuwait		1,137.0	1,201.0	4,363.0	1.1	38.1
Norway		2,943.0	3,706.0	4,292.0	4.7	3.7

Note: (W) = Weighted Mean (U) = Unweighted Mean (M) = Median

Table 14 (cont.). Public Recurrent Expenditures on Education per Pupil

		Expenditures (US$)			Growth (%)	
		1975	1980	1984	1975-1980	1980-1984
Secondary						
Low Income Countries	(W)	52.8	67.4	91.9	5.0	8.1
	(U)	284.1	176.6	103.5	(9.1)	(12.5)
	(M)	191.0	156.0	111.5	(4.0)	(8.1)
Selected Countries with Low Expenditures						
Bangladesh		-	12.0	15.0	-	5.7
Haiti		-	42.0	21.0	-	(15.9)
Selected Countries with High Expenditures						
Central African Republic		182.0	-	58.0	-	-
Mali		-	156.0	129.0	-	(4.6)
** China		53.0	69.0	97.0	-	-
** India		42.0	-	-	-	-
Lower-Middle Income Countries	(W)	187.5	200.3	184.0	1.3	(2.1)
	(U)	287.2	300.0	211.8	0.9	(8.3)
	(M)	230.0	232.5	173.5	0.2	(7.1)
Selected Countries with Low Expenditures						
Bolivia		58.0	91.0	54.0	9.4	(12.2)
Dominican Republic		66.0	63.0	69.0	(0.9)	2.3
Selected Countries with High Expenditures						
Côte D'Ivoire		814.0	801.0	-	(0.3)	-
Turkey		-	-	1,585.0	-	-
Upper-Middle Income Countries	(W)	298.5	243.2	358.7	(4.0)	10.2
	(U)	397.5	436.1	388.0	1.9	(2.9)
	(M)	271.0	302.0	417.0	2.2	8.4
Selected Countries with Low Expenditures						
Chile		171.0	311.0	-	12.7	-
Mexico		262.0	150.0	90.0	(10.6)	(12.0)
Selected Countries with High Expenditures						
Iran, Islamic Republic of		615.0	-	567.0	-	-
Ireland		998.0	1,243.0	1,280.0	4.5	0.7
High Income Countries	(W)	2,010.5	2,197.5	1,756.0	1.8	(5.5)
	(U)	2,073.0	2,221.4	2,320.6	1.4	1.1
	(M)	1,599.0	1,646.5	1,811.0	0.6	2.4
Selected Countries with Low Expenditures						
Hong Kong		235.0	403.0	603.0	11.4	10.6
Israel		1,483.0	224.0	-	(31.5)	-
Selected Countries with High Expenditures						
Kuwait		1,569.0	1,398.0	1,877.0	(2.3)	7.6
Norway		1,779.0	2,033.0	2,051.0	2.7	0.2

Note: (W) = Weighted Mean (U) = Unweighted Mean (M) = Median

Table 14 (cont.). Public Recurrent Expenditures on Education per Pupil

		Expenditures (US$)			Growth (%)	
		1975	1980	1984	1975-1980	1980-1984
Tertiary						
Low Income Countries	(W)	212.1	825.9	677.1	31.2	(4.8)
	(U)	2,704.4	2,071.1	1,167.0	(5.2)	(13.4)
	(M)	2,298.0	1,834.0	1,067.0	(4.4)	(12.7)
Selected Countries with Low Expenditures						
Bangladesh		-	106.0	78.0	-	(7.4)
Haiti		494.0	419.0	278.0	(3.2)	(9.7)
Selected Countries with High Expenditures						
Central African Republic		4,278.0	-	1,745.0	-	-
Mali		2,298.0	6,196.0	1,287.0	21.9	(32.5)
** China		837.0	857.0	845.0	0.5	(0.4)
** India		99.0	-	-	0.0	0.0
Lower-Middle Income Countries	(W)	858.7	1,110.9	3,124.9	5.3	29.5
	(U)	2,686.8	2,025.4	2,070.7	(5.5)	0.6
	(M)	1,189.0	1,050.0	1,347.0	(2.5)	6.4
Selected Countries with Low Expenditures						
Bolivia		310.0	-	-	-	-
Dominican Republic		-	-	-	-	-
Selected Countries with High Expenditures						
Côte D'Ivoire		6,969.0	3,287.0	-	(14.0)	-
Turkey		-	11,787.0	6,453.0	-	(14.0)
Upper-Middle Income Countries	(W)	1,924.1	1,280.5	918.4	(7.8)	(8.0)
	(U)	2,852.1	2,029.0	1,617.3	(6.6)	(5.5)
	(M)	880.5	1,053.0	768.0	3.6	(7.6)
Selected Countries with Low Expenditures						
Chile		959.0	2,119.0	1,167.0	17.2	(13.9)
Mexico		555.0	1,113.0	931.0	14.9	(4.4)
Selected Countries with High Expenditures						
Iran, Islamic Republic of		19,246.0	-	5,232.0	-	-
Ireland		2,802.0	3,063.0	2,731.0	1.8	(2.8)
High Income Countries	(W)	4,018.9	3,243.1	2,494.4	(4.2)	(6.4)
	(U)	4,392.9	4,226.6	3,834.9	(0.8)	(2.4)
	(M)	3,831.5	3,446.0	3,460.0	(2.1)	0.1
Selected Countries with Low Expenditures						
Hong Kong		1,533.0	3,411.0	2,539.0	17.3	(7.1)
Israel		-	392.0	407.0	-	0.9
Selected Countries with High Expenditures						
Kuwait		9,365.0	7,345.0	8,550.0	(4.7)	3.9
Norway		4,696.0	5,189.0	4,765.0	2.0	(2.1)

Note: (W) = Weighted Mean   (U) = Unweighted Mean   (M) = Median

Table 15. Public Recurrent Expenditures on Education per Pupil as a Percentage of GNP Per Capita

		Primary			Secondary			Tertiary		
		1975	1980	1984	1975	1980	1984	1975	1980	1984
Low-Income Countries	(W)	16.0	15.6	12.5	102.7	68.7	37.2	9.9	8.1	6.0
	(U)	17.4	15.8	14.9	107.9	71.9	43.4	10.6	9.7	6.9
	(M)	13.5	13.5	15.0	75.5	60.0	29.0	9.7	6.8	5.8
Selected Countries with Low Expenditures										
Bangladesh		4.0	5.0	7.0	-	10.0	12.0	-	0.9	0.6
Haiti		6.0	6.0	5.0	-	12.0	7.0	1.7	1.2	0.9
Selected Countries with High Expenditures										
Ethiopia		35.0	19.0	23.0	-	-	-	-	13.0	14.0
Mali		-	32.0	40.0	-	92.0	87.0	15.8	36.7	8.7
** China		-	-	-	28.0	30.0	32.0	4.5	3.8	2.7
** India		11.0	10.0	-	19.0	-	-	0.5	-	-
Lower-Middle Income Countries	(W)	11.0	14.0	13.6	31.3	32.4	32.8	3.2	2.0	1.7
	(U)	13.0	14.7	14.0	37.4	39.9	35.6	3.4	2.2	1.8
	(M)	10.0	12.0	11.0	19.0	20.5	21.0	1.1	0.9	1.2
Selected Countries with Low Expenditures										
Dominican Republic		4.0	3.0	5.0	7.0	6.0	7.0	-	-	-
Syrian Arab Republic		5.0	5.0	7.0	10.0	10.0	9.0	0.6	0.5	0.7
Selected Countries with High Expenditures										
Côte d'Ivoire		21.0	21.0	-	115.0	104.0	-	9.9	4.3	-
Morocco		20.0	16.0	19.0	74.0	59.0	48.0	2.3	1.6	1.8
Upper-Middle Income Countries	(W)	11.2	13.2	16.0	14.3	15.5	17.2	1.1	0.7	0.7
	(U)	12.1	12.9	15.6	14.1	16.0	16.1	0.8	0.8	0.6
	(M)	7.0	10.0	14.0	15.0	13.0	12.5	0.4	0.4	0.5
Selected Countries with Low Expenditures										
Greece		6.0	7.0	-	7.0	8.0	-	0.3	0.3	-
Mexico		6.0	5.0	4.0	16.0	8.0	5.0	0.3	0.6	0.5
Selected Countries with High Expenditures										
Iran, Islamic Rep. of		7.0	21.0	-	14.0	-	-	4.4	-	-
Ireland		15.0	12.0	18.0	23.0	25.0	26.0	0.6	0.6	0.6

Note: (W) = Weighted Mean   (U) = Unweighted Mean   (M) = Median.

Table 15 (cont.). Public Recurrent Expenditures on Education per Pupil as a Percentage of GNP Per Capita

		Primary			Secondary			Tertiary		
		1975	1980	1984	1975	1980	1984	1975	1980	1984
High-Income Countries	(W)	19.6	17.2	19.8	24.8	23.3	24.4	0.5	0.4	0.4
	(U)	18.4	16.3	17.9	23.2	21.8	22.9	0.5	0.4	0.4
	(M)	14.5	13.5	15.5	20.0	16.5	21.0	0.5	0.4	0.4
Selected Countries with Low Expenditures										
Israel		12.0	2.0	-	29.0	4.0	-	-	0.1	0.1
Singapore		7.0	7.0	8.0	11.0	14.0	11.0	0.4	0.4	0.6
Selected Countries with High Expenditures										
Norway		29.0	30.0	32.0	17.0	16.0	15.0	0.5	0.4	0.4
Sweden		29.0	44.0	44.0	14.0	15.0	16.0	0.4	0.3	0.3

Note: (W) = Weighted Mean (U) = Unweighted Mean (M) = Median.

3.7   Comparing rate of return estimates with enrollment expansion also suggests that many countries are investing in education consistently with the way that economic payoff data suggest they should be. Other countries are not. Generally, these countries are overinvesting in higher education and underinvesting in primary education -- in many cases, underinvesting particularly in girls' primary education.

The Educational Spending Crisis

3.8   There are also well-developed data on educational spending, by country and over time. Table 12, page 27, shows that slower economic growth in the 1980s has been accompanied by cuts in the percentage of GNP going to public education -- this, after increases in the 1970s. Table 13, page 28, suggests (looking at the unweighted means) that all but the low-income countries have accomplished this cut in spending on education by cutting the percentage of public budgets going to education; that is, by shifting resources to other public spending objectives.

3.9   The net result of these policies is shown in Tables 14, page 29, and 15, page 32 — the growth of spending-per-pupil and the amount spent per pupil at different levels of education as a percentage of GNP per capita. Again, focusing on the unweighted means in Table 14, the results show that in low-income countries, where spending-per-pupil in primary schools is very low, this spending declined in 1975-84, especially in 1980-84. At the secondary level, where spending-per-pupil was the same in 1975, on average, as in lower middle-income countries, cuts were even more rapid, although all these cuts and particularly the cuts in higher education could be rationalized in terms of what spending-per-pupil "should" be in terms of income per capita (Table 15). The "right" amount of spending-per-pupil is a crucial issue in developing educational quality criteria. But in general, if the U.S./European model of schooling is to be duplicated in low-income countries, it is likely that per-pupil spending as a ratio of income per capita will be higher than in higher-income countries, primarily because of the greater scarcity of teacher skills.

3.10   It is clear from these data that the 1970s and especially the 1980s have been periods of declining growth of real public spending on education, particularly per-pupil-spending. Between 1975 and 1980, for example, this growth rate was lower than the growth of national income for more than one-third of a sample of 55 countries (World Bank, 1986).

3.11   The trend reflects two mutually reinforcing factors: (a) the decline in many countries of overall public budgets in real terms in the wake of the two major world recessions of 1974-75 and 1980-83 combined with severe foreign debt crises in Latin America, Sub-Saharan Africa, and some countries in Asia and -- in the Middle East -- lower oil prices (Haddad and Demsky, 1987); and (b) the large proportion of government budgets devoted to education, especially in Sub-Saharan Africa and Latin America. With tight finances, intersectoral competition for resources seems to have put pressure on social spending, particularly education. This has resulted in a declining budget share for public education in most of the world's regions. Although there are some important exceptions to this trend (China, the Republic of Korea, and Taiwan), many countries have experienced much larger declines than the average figures suggest. In some countries, furthermore, declines in the percentage of the public budget going to education have been accompanied by increases in the proportion spent on the military (Carnoy, 1986).

3.12   Statistics on the private flow of funds to education are scarce, but existing data show that as a share of total national educational expenditures, private spending has also declined in most developing countries (World Bank, 1986).

3.13   The decline in growth of educational spending goes counter to two other trends: continued rapid growth of the school-age population in many of the world's lowest-income countries and an increase in average cost-per-pupil as the average level of education attended increases from low-cost primary to higher-cost secondary and university. Most Sub-Saharan African and particularly Latin American countries have attempted to deal with this impasse by reducing real spending-per-pupil at all levels, especially in Latin America at the tertiary level (see Heller and Cheasty, 1984, and Table 15, page 32). Others have not kept up with school-age population growth, increasing the absolute number of primary school-age children not in school.

3.14   Many Asian countries, however, have increased per-pupil spending in the 1980s (although not as rapidly as in the 1970s) even as the percentage of their public spending on education has continued to decline. This suggests that in higher economic growth regions with low rates of population increase, the problems of educational finance have rather different dimensions than in the lower economic growth/higher population growth regions Sub-Saharan Africa and Latin America. And in many Latin American countries, relatively high primary school survival rates and secondary school enrollment rates mean that the educational crisis is largely one of expanding the secondary and tertiary levels rather than the primary level (Brazil is a notable exception among the larger countries). It also suggests that the economic development gap between the more rapidly developing countries in Asia and the lower-income countries in Sub-Saharan Africa and Latin America is bound to increase as education expands in the faster-growing countries and falls behind in the stagnant ones. Even the larger, higher-income countries in Latin America stand to hurt their future technological modernization as their educational systems fail to keep pace with development requirements.

3.15   These data also indicate that although the cost of providing all children access to good education is great, the goal is within reach. If the economic growth rate in the low-income countries (excluding China and India, whose universal primary school enrollment should not be a financial problem) is 3.2 percent, and in the low middle-income countries, 3.0 percent, between 1985 and 2000, recurrent expenditures for primary education would have to reach 2.4 and 1.9 percent of GNP, respectively, in order to achieve 100 percent enrollment. In

Sub-Saharan Africa, countries already spend a high percentage of their public budget on education -- they need policies to more efficiently allocate resources and diversify their resource base, as well as new, highly effective approaches to teaching and learning. In South Asia, the problem is mainly underfinancing of education, but countries such as Bangladesh also need new approaches to delivering education.

4

Lessons from World Bank and Other Donor Experience with Assistance to Education and Training

4.1   The World Bank has been investing in education for 25 years. It has made loans for over 350 projects in 92 countries. Operations Evaluation Department (OED) project completion reports are available for 161 projects, and audits of these completed projects are also available. In addition, the Bank has done sector performance analyses and summaries of experiences in education. Therefore, a vast amount of Bank experience in educational investment has been extensively chronicled and assessed.

4.2   Other donors have also invested heavily in developing countries' education. These include: (i) the regional development banks -- Asian, African, and Inter-American; (ii) the bilateral agencies -- USAID, CIDA, SIDA, ODA, NORAD, Canadian IDRC, DANIDA, and French Cooperation; (iii) the international agencies -- UNESCO, UNICEF, and ILO; and (iv) the foundations -- primarily Ford and Rockefeller. Their experiences have also been chronicled and many evaluated.

Total Education Sector Lending by Multilateral and Bilateral Agencies

4.3   The World Bank plays a singularly important role in international lending for education. Since the 1970s it has been the largest single provider of external funding for educational development, providing approximately 15 percent of all official external aid to education (Table 16). Since bilateral aid is largely for technical assistance, the Bank is by far the larger lender for capital investments. In many countries the Bank is the major source of educational policy advice, and other agencies increasingly follow the Bank's lead in such policy and lending. Therefore, its experiences and the policy implications of those experiences carry particularly significant weight in how educational development and lending proceeds worldwide. With more than US$4 billion flowing to developing countries annually for education and training, the World Bank will make an important impact on educational change -- hence economic development -- in the coming decade.

History of Bank Investments in Education and Training

4.4   The World Bank loaned US$11.2 billion dollars for education in 1962-87 through 355 education projects. Although the absolute amount of education and training loans has varied from year to year, in relative terms, they have stayed at about six percent of total annual loans (Table 16), somewhat less than other multilateral agencies and much less relatively than bilateral lending agencies.

Table 16. Comparative Flow of Education Aid, 1980-86
(US$ Millions)

Year	World Bank		Other Multilateral Agencies [a]		Bilateral Aid from Member Countries of the DAC of the OECD [b]		Total		
	Educ. Lending	% of Total Lending	Aid to Educ.	% of Total Aid	Aid to Educ.	% of Total Aid	Aid to Educ.	% of Total Aid	World Bank % of Total Educ. Aid
1980	440.1	3.8	256.7	5.8	3,394.8	13.9	4,091.6	10.2	16.8
1981	747.9	6.1	296.4	5.9	2,595.9	11.4	3,640.2	9.1	20.6
1982	526.4	4.0	468.1	8.7	2,542.6	11.1	3,537.1	8.6	14.9
1983	547.9	3.8	498.9	8.2	2,755.7	11.7	3,802.5	8.6	14.4
1984	701.9	4.5	331.3	4.8	3,213.6	12.2	4,246.8	8.7	16.5
1985	936.8	6.5	338.2	5.4	4,997.7	13.0	4,125.5	9.7	14.9
1986	839.5	5.1	453.8	6.8	2,858.9	10.9	4,702.9	9.6	20.2

[a] Includes African Development Bank, Asian Development Bank, Inter-American Development Bank, Islamic Development Bank, UNICEF and UNESCO.
[b] Includes loans, grants, etc. (excludes contributions to multilateral organizations).

Table 17. Distribution of Lending for Education and Training by Region
(US$ Millions)

Period	Africa	Asia	LAC	EMENA	Total
Total	2,466	4,235	1,529	3,011	11,241
FY63-68	206	89	61	123	479
FY69-73	577	479	233	433	1,722
FY74-78	537	516	421	742	2,216
FY79-83	538	1,381	367	709	2,995
FY84-88	561	1,770	447	1,004	3,782

Table 18. Distribution of Investments by Type of Curricula and Level of Education

Type	FY63-76	FY77-86
Total	100%	100%
General Education	43%	53%
Primary	6%	22%
Secondary	20%	10%
Nonformal Literacy	1%	-
Post-Secondary	4%	14%
Teacher Training	11%	6%
Vocational Education	51%	44%
Secondary	23%	6%
Post-Secondary	16%	24%
Nonformal Skill Training	11%	13%
Teacher Training	1%	1%
Non-Allocated	7%	3%

Table 19. Pattern of Education Project Expenditures

Type	FY79-81	FY84-86
Total	100%	100%
Civil Works	55%	44%
Equipment & Furniture	29%	31%
Technical Assistance	7%	10%
Other Expenditures	9%	15%

Table 20. Education Subsector Reviews

FY84-85	Relation of sector work and completion reporting to education projects' preparation
FY85	Effectiveness of varied training modes in provision of project-related training components
FY86-87	Performance review of free-standing vocational training projects in both education and non-education sectors
FY88	Review of experience with policy-based lending in education projects

Table 21. Reviews of Bank Experience in the Education Sector

Primary Education	Examination of Bank performance in provision of primary education through 68 projects, at a total project cost of US$1.4 billion.
Secondary Education	Analysis of Bank experience with specialized secondary school curricula supported in 79 education projects through FY63-79 that attempted to "vocationalize" part of a general secondary school curricula.
University Education	Review of Bank experience with lending for university level education in 120 education projects through FY63-88 (to be completed December 1988).
Adult Literacy	Evaluation of policy and experience in 92 Bank education projects during FY63-85 that taught adult literacy and basic skill training through project components outside of the formal school system.
Vocational Education	*Industry*: Analysis of the performance of Bank investments in vocational training for industry through 76 projects in FY63-87 covering US$4.7 billion project costs. *Commerce*: Evaluation of Bank experience with 43 investments in commerce training (to be completed January 1989).
Distance Education	Review of Bank experience in 32 distance education components (i.e. radio, television, correspondence courses) during FY63-85.
Textbooks	Review of Bank experience through 48 project components in FY63-83 for the preparation, provision and distribution of learning materials and teacher guides.
Teacher Training	Study of the effectiveness of 149 teacher training components for primary and secondary teachers in Bank education projects, covering 9 percent of education lending in FY63-84.
Sector Management	Analysis of education sector management components through 17 education projects in 12 countries.
Monitoring & Evaluation	Examination of three case studies of Bank education projects with successful monitoring and evaluation components.
Sector Loans	Evaluation of seven education sector loans to identify procedural issues for future preparation of sector loans and sectoral adjustment projects.
Educational Change	*General Experience:* Examination of the performance of Bank project components aimed at educational quality improvement and change, through FY63-84, totalling US$6.4 billion of total project costs (60% of all education projects costs). *Teaching:* In-depth review of 21 education project components for teacher training designed to support the implementation of project components for educational quality improvement. *Textbooks:* In-depth review of 11 education project components for textbook production and/or provision designed to support the implementation of project components for educational quality improvements.

4.5 The focus of the Bank's education lending has shifted over time across three dimensions: regionally, by level of education, and by type of project components. The Bank has moved from an early emphasis on Sub-Saharan Africa to a much higher percentage of lending to Asia and the Middle East (Table 17). The Bank has also shifted from a heavy emphasis on general and vocational secondary education in the FY63-76 period to much greater focus on primary and post-secondary education (general and vocational) in the FY77-88 period (Table 18). This was consistent with the objectives set out in the 1980 Education Sector Policy Paper, emphasizing investments in basic education in low-income countries, and secondary and higher education in those middle-income countries where basic education has been established. There was also a much more gradual change from lending for buildings to technical assistance and other expenditures (Table 19, page 39).

4.6 Investments by the Bank in education and training are carried out through two main channels: (1) Education projects, which lend directly for general and technical education at primary, secondary, and tertiary levels, and vocational education and training for specific occupational fields; and (2) Project-related training (PRT), i.e., training components in non-education projects (indirect lending for education), aimed at ensuring that project objectives are not constrained by lack of adequately skilled manpower.

Education and Training Department/Division Reviews:
Reviews of Education and Training Operations

4.7 Annual reviews of the Bank's operations in education lending and project-related training components (which averages US$600 million or about six percent of overall Bank annual lending) have been prepared by the human resources sector staff in the PPR complex (and by their pre-Reorganization forerunners -- Operations Policy Staff) each year since FY77. Changes in regional lending patterns are reviewed, and any fluctuations are then examined within the context of three-year or five-year lending patterns.

4.8 Project costs are also compiled by: (1) level of education (primary, secondary, university, and vocational training); (2) curricula (basic/general and technical/vocational); and (3) category of expenditure (civil works, equipment & furniture, technical assistance). Again, fluctuations are reviewed within an annual and a three-year or five-year context.

Table 22. OED Project Completion/Audit Reports in the Education Sector

Region	Total No. of Completion/Audit Reports	Countries with More than One Completion/Audit Report		
		No. of Reports		
		2	3	4
Africa	64	15	4	3
Asia	29	2	-	5 [a]
EMENA	35	6	2	3
LAC	33	11	3	-
Total	161	34	9	11

[a] Includes Indonesia and the Philippines, with five and six reports, respectively.

4.9   For the past five years these annual reviews have also been used as an opportunity to concentrate on subsector issues of interest to operational staff:

Education and Training Department/Division Reviews:
Reviews of Sectoral Performance

4.10   In addition to annual reviews of lending, the Bank has also conducted reviews of its experience in important subsectors of education lending, as shown in Table 21, page 40.

Operations Evaluation Department Reviews:
Reviews of Education Project Performance

4.11   OED has conducted project performance evaluations for 161 completed education projects, in the form of Project Completion Reports and Project Performance Audit Reports. In addition, OED has prepared Impact Evaluation Reports on education projects in Colombia, the Philippines and Thailand. These performance reviews cut across the many levels and types of projects in which the Bank has invested. A particular benefit of these reviews lies in the 11 countries where the Bank has had "lessons learned" from a series of at least four completed projects (Table 22, page 41).

Operations Evaluation Department Reviews:
Reviews of Sectoral Performance

4.12   In addition to reviewing discrete education projects, OED has conducted reviews of sectoral operations on: (1) the formal education sector (1978); (2) the project-related training sector (1982); and (3) the impact of 15 years of Bank education investments in Korea (1985).

Education Sector Performance Review by Other Donor Agencies

4.13   Complementary to the Bank's internal evaluations of its project and sectoral performance in education, many other agencies have a long history of involvement in the education and training sector. In particular, two other UN agencies -- UNESCO and UNICEF, the bilateral agencies -- the United States Agency for International Development (USAID), the Swedish International Development Authority (SIDA), the Canadian International Development Agency (CIDA), and the Canadian International Development Research Centre (IDRC), and independent agencies such as the Rockefeller and Ford Foundations have a wealth of experience. Collaboration with these agencies is a common experience throughout the Bank's activities in education lending, and some of their internal evaluation resources available to the Bank are shown in Table 23.

Table 23. Evaluations of Education and Training Activities Available from other Agencies

Agency	Number of Years Involved in Education and Training	Available Evaluation Reports
UNESCO	43	75
IDRC	11	110
SIDA	23	160
ROCKEFELLER	13	130
UNICEF	25	105
USAID	27	90

5

Policy Issues and Directions

5.1   An extensive body of analyses is available assessing the impact of various interventions on the effectiveness and efficiency of education and the learning process. These analyses are divided into seven topics: (i) skill formation (vocational education and training); (ii) the quality and efficiency of education; (iii) technology in education; (iv) sector management; (v) science education; (vi) higher education and technology transfer; and (vii) educational financial reforms.

Vocational and Academic Secondary Education

5.2   When educational planners in developing countries consider investing in education for economic development, many think of vocational education and training, especially at the secondary level (Bacchus, 1988). It is such directly job skills-related education that many planners believe to be most connected to increasing economic output. Vocational education's popularity among policymakers also stems in part from its social function. It tends to be substituted for general education for students who do not succeed academically. Policymakers want to prepare these less academically able students for some sort of practical work and to reduce pressure on higher education by making vocational education terminal. It is precisely for this reason that there has never been much enthusiasm among students or their parents for such education, except as a second-best way to avoid unemployment (Foster, 1966).

5.3   There are now a large number of studies -- many of them carried out for the World Bank (Picciotto, 1965; Fuller, 1970; Arriagazzi, 1972; Borus, 1977; Godfrey, 1977; Castro, 1979; Levine, 1979; Puryear, 1979; Psacharopoulos, 1982; Cohen, 1983; Ziderman, 1988; Grootaert, 1988) -- which challenge the notion that skill training in vocational schools is the best educational investment strategy for economic development, or even the most cost-effective way to impart those skills (see Table 24). They recommend alternative strategies. Metcalf (1985) summarizes this research. The studies show, he argues, that although there is economic justification for public intervention in the training effort (as evidenced by reasonably high rates of return to vocational training), training carried out in industrial institutes and vocational secondary schools appears to be less cost-effective than more informal, firm-based training; short-courses appear to have a bigger payoff than longer courses of training; and the payoff to quasi-institutional vocational training may be higher for those who have completed primary school than for those who have completed secondary. Grootaert's analysis of vocational education in the Côte d'Ivoire (1988) confirms the low return to all levels of formal vocational education, but shows that returns to higher secondary vocational education are not as low as those to post-primary vocational education.

Table 24. Vocational-Technical Education and Training versus Academic Education: Selected Empirical Studies in Developing Countries

Study	Data	Results
Foster (1966)	Students in Ghana	Classic study which argues that all education is vocational but that "vocational" education (VTE) and training is considered second-rate because it leads to lower status occupations than academic track. This is known as the "vocational education fallacy."
Metcalf (1985)	Review of studies in a number of different countries	Rate of return to vocational training is high enough to justify investment. Shorter courses have a higher payoff. Informal firm-based training is more cost-effective than vocational secondary schools. In South America, vocational training for primary school completers has higher payoff than to secondary school completers. VTE in industry-linked institutions has higher payoff than in non-affiliated institutions.
Fuller (1970)	Survey of workers in two electrical machinery plants in Bangalore, India	Productivity of in-school vocational trained workers is 9% lower than in-firm trained workers and costs of in-school training are higher.
Godfrey (1977)	400+ exam candidates in Kenya, 1973	Graduates with school vocational training are 14-25% less likely to pass government craft tests than those with no such training.
Psacharopoulos (1988)	Six firms in Lima, Peru in 1982	Short SENATI courses gave high returns, whereas two-year SENATI courses had low returns.
Castro (1979)	Brazil--Sao Paulo & Rio manufacturing sector, large firms, 1970	Social rates of return of SENAI own-firm training were higher for those workers with completed secondary education than those with junior high. Rates rather high.
Puryear (1979)	Bogota, Colombia 1965-67 SENA graduates, sampled in 1972	Three-year SENA graduates earn, over a SENA apprenticeship sample as a whole, 48% more than equivalent non-SENA graduates, but this SENA effect is smaller for those with more than six years of schooling.
Psacharapoulos and Loxley (1985)	Follow-up survey of graduates from diversified and non-diversified secondary in Colombia or Tanzania	There is no labor advantage to graduates from vocational courses, either in terms of success in finding employment or in pay levels when employed either in Colombia or Tanzania. Costs of programs are also similar.

Table 24 (cont.). Vocational-Technical Education and Training versus Academic Education: Selected Empirical Studies in Developing Countries

Study	Data	Results
Hinchliffe (1983)	Tanzania	Total annual unit recurrent costs are 19% higher in agricultural biased schools, 13% higher in technical biased schools, and 9% higher in commerce biased schools compared with academic schools.
Cummings, et al. (1985)	Kenya	Staffing costs are twice and and capital costs are five times for industrial education subjects as for those of classroom subjects.
Tibi (1986)	Thailand	Recurrent costs of agricultural colleges were 98% higher and three kinds of technical colleges were 54% higher than in professional colleges.
Komenan (1987)	Ivory Coast 1984 labor force survey	Technical education has higher payoff than general education at every level of schooling, but costs of technical education are much higher (2.5 times higher at secondary level).
Grootaert (1988)	Ivory Coast, Living Standards Survey, 1985	Social rates of return are low to VTE, but higher to post-secondary than to post-primary VTE, and higher than to apprenticeship training. Private rates of return are much higher because of large public costs. Rates are also higher to those outside of Abidjan.
Moock and Bellew (1988)	Male urban sub-sample of Peru Living Standards Survey, 1985/86	Monetary returns are generally similar to VTE and academic stream graduates, except for self-employed outside Lima. Unit costs are also similar for VTE and academic streams.
Chung (1987)	Hong Kong census, 1976 and 1981	Returns to VTE are higher than to general education, but significant only for the rapidly-growing electrical and commercial sectors.
Min and Tsang (1987)	Survey of workers in Beijing General Auto Industry Company	Productivity of workers with VTE 7% higher than those with general secondary education.
Ziderman (1988)	Israel, 1983 census	Vocational secondary schooling more cost-effective than general education for those who do not go on to post-secondary education, especially for those who work in occupations related to course of study.

Table 24 (cont.). **Vocational-Technical Education and Training versus Academic Education: Selected Empirical Studies in Developing Countries**

Study	Data	Results
Lee, C. (1985)	South Korea secondary graduates	In-plant vocational training is more cost-effective than training in vocational schools.
Chin-Aleong (1988)	Trinidad & Tobago labor force survey	Specialized craft students found jobs more quickly and earned better salaries than did academic students or those with pretechnician courses.
Schiefelbein & Farrell (1982)	Sample of eighth grade Chilean students	Tracking students into vocational curricula where academic achievement is not emphasized will lower student achievement.
Noah and Middleton (1988)	Secondary data from two provinces in China: Lingoning and Hubeii	China is attempting to reach a 50-50 general to vocational education enrollment mix by 1990. But they conclude that in order to meet the demands of economy, China needs to shift away from apprenticeship-VTE to in-school VTE.

5.4   Recent research by Psacharopoulos and Loxley (1985) on Colombia and Tanzania, Lauglo and Narman (1988) in Kenya and Chin-Aleong (1988) in Trinidad and Tobago suggests that the cost-effectiveness of introducing pre-vocational subjects in traditional secondary schools (diversified secondary education) is also low if their goal is to help school-leavers find a source of livelihood under difficult labor market conditions. There may be other reasons for diversifying secondary schools -- such as giving students some experience in manual work or attempting to provide greater equity in access to academic secondary education, but pre-vocational courses may be an expensive way to achieve these goals.

5.5   There is some evidence that schooling is complementary to in-firm and project training. Fuller found in his Bangalore, India study (1970) that extra schooling seems to be an important prerequisite for on-the-job learning. In a more approximate estimation, Mingat (1984) sampled 52 worldwide agricultural projects supported by the World Bank in the early 1980s, and found that the returns to project-related training are larger, the higher the adult literacy rate in the country.

5.6   More than twenty years of studying vocational education therefore raises serious questions about the economic value of investing in expensive vocational schooling, especially where such schooling is not directly connected to an employment situation (as in some of the Latin American systems such as SENA (Colombia) and SENAI (Brazil)). Vocational education is much more expensive than academic, and, if unconnected to an employer or group of employers, does not appear to give graduates any advantage in finding work or earning higher wages.

5.7   However, under certain conditions, vocational education may have a high payoff. In-firm training or training in institutions with an employment connection (SENA and SENAI, for example; see also Min and Tsang, 1987, for the higher productivity of workers with vocational education in China) may yield a reasonably high benefit-cost ratio. Recent research in Hong Kong (Chung, 1987) and an extensive review of World Bank investment in vocational education and training (Middleton and Demsky, 1988) also suggest that investment in vocational education in those skills relevant to rapidly growing industries and, more generally, in industrially dynamic economies, have a higher payoff than to academic education. Chung shows that workers who graduated from vocational education institutions that prepared them for careers in such rapidly growing industries were more likely to work in the jobs for which they were trained and earned higher wages than their counterparts with academic education.

5.8   All this suggests a more selective approach to investing in vocational education and training, focusing much more on in-firm and firm-connected or industry-connected programs, and on those related to rapidly growing sectors. In the middle-income countries, training investments should support the introduction of new technologies and continuous industrial restructuring -- which means upgrading the general knowledge and specific skills of the labor force. General education would usually take place off-the-job, but much of the skill training can be industry-based. For this purpose, technologies have been developed in recent years using advances in the electronic media. Few developing countries are adequately exploiting the potential of these technologies.

5.9   Low-income countries -- with weak enterprises and stagnant demand for skills -- require a different training strategy. Pre-employment training is more important, since enterprises themselves have little training capacity, and this training should be more generic, focusing on general academic preparation in science, mathematics, and language (Heyneman, 1987), which makes workers more trainable, and on self-employment and entrepreneurship (Komenan, 1987).

5.10   There are also still a number of unanswered questions, such as the relative adaptability of academically and vocationally-trained workers to work situations involving rapid technological change. This is particularly important when we consider that the organization of industrial production is undergoing significant and rapid change and that many developing countries are seeking high technology transfer. The evidence suggesting that academic schooling is complementary to on-the-job learning (Fuller, 1970) indicates that those workers with more academic skills may be more adaptable and easier to retrain. But more research is needed to confirm such results.

The Quality and Efficiency of Education

5.11   Students in low-income countries are not only getting less years of education, they are learning less in each of those years than students in higher-income countries: mathematics and science scores are lower in low-income and most middle-income countries than in the NICs and industrialized countries (Heyneman and Loxley, 1983; Table 25, page 51). Further, the knowledge gap may be growing: measured in terms of spending-per-pupil and the ratio of pupils to teachers, quality of education has declined in the lowest-income countries and improved in the middle-income countries; and developing countries with higher enrollment rates in 1970 were more able to improve quality through 1980 than countries that experienced rapidly growing enrollments in the 1970s (Fuller, 1987).

5.12   Improving access to and the quality of basic education is a priority in almost every low-income and middle-income country. In addition to being a highly productive investment in its own right, an effective basic education provides the literacy and numeric skills that are necessary for all further education and training. In many countries, particular attention has to be paid to girls' education, which, even with school quality improvements, may not expand quickly without special attention to community and family barriers that impede girls' attendance.

5.13 Improved access and quality are inextricably linked: about 60 million of 400 million primary and secondary school places are occupied by repeaters. As much as 20 percent of education budgets is spent to teach repeaters and future drop-outs. In many countries, reducing repetition and improving quality across the board will require not only a different philosophy about the role of primary schooling (having all pupils reach relatively high standards of learning and achievement rather than acting as a gatekeeper-selector to keep most pupils from completing their primary education), but also additional budget allocations, and more efficient allocation of educational spending.

5.14 There is some evidence that improving student achievement in school or increasing school inputs (teacher quality) may have a higher economic payoff (as measured by increased earnings of school-leavers) than investing in additional years of schooling (Carnoy, Sack and Thias, 1977; Behrman and Birdsall, 1983), and that improved school inputs may have more of an effect on student achievement in developing than in developed countries (Heyneman and Loxley, 1983; Solmon, 1985).

5.15 Assuming that the quality of school inputs could be improved through additional resources, how can schooling best be made more effective to increase student achievement? Since the United States' "Coleman Report" (1966), a large number of studies have addressed this issue in both developed and developing countries. The results of these "educational production functions" vary widely and are fraught with methodological problems, not least of which are that it is unclear what unit of production to use (individual pupil, classroom, school, school district) and whether the relevant unit of production is maximizing academic achievement or some other output (Carnoy, Sack, and Thias, 1977). Neither do any of the studies specify an underlying theory of learning that would define the nature of the school inputs-academic achievement relationship: they all assume that teacher inputs can be measured by teacher characteristics (education, experience, and aptitude), ignoring the way or the degree to which those characteristics are engaged in the teaching-learning process (Levin, 1980).

5.16 Because of these limitations, educational production studies have produced inconclusive and often contradictory findings (Fuller, 1987). Nonetheless, some consistent general findings do emerge from these studies (see Table 25, page 51). First, variation in school inputs, such as teacher experience, teacher motivation, the presence of textbooks, homework, and time spent in school during the year do contribute to varying pupil achievement, even when family background differences are accounted for (Summers and Wolfe, 1977; Alexander and Simmons, 1978; Heyneman and Loxley, 1983; Fuller, 1987). Second, although the studies explain little of the total variance in individual achievement (which reflects the complexity of the teaching-learning process), they have been more successful in explaining variations in achievement among schools than within schools. Third, in lower-income developing countries, the fact that there is much wider variation in school inputs than in middle-income and developed countries means that upgrading the amount of school inputs and the quality of the teaching process at the low end may raise academic achievement substantially (see also Zuzovsky, 1987, for a similar effect on low achievers in Israel).

5.17 However, educational production function studies have not been able to tell us accurately which school inputs have larger and smaller effects on achievement. Neither have they been particularly useful in identifying which inputs are more cost-effective than others -- although "size" effects of the inputs are often a product of such studies, they rarely measure costs of inputs (for a review of cost-effectiveness of school inputs, see Lockheed and Hanushek, 1987).

Table 25. Improving the Quality of Education: Selected Empirical Studies in Developing Countries

Study	Data Base	Results
Alexander and Simmons (1978)	A number of country studies relating school inputs and family background variables to school achievement	Found no consistent influence of school effects net of family background
Fuller (1987)	Large number of studies relating school achievement to school variables in developing countries	Variety of school inputs do contribute to pupil achievement, but studies tend to be atheoretical and miss understanding process of schooling.
Lockheed and Hanushek (1987)	Studies that provide both effect-size and cost data on specific school inputs. Six inputs reviewed, including radio, textbooks, and teacher training	Radio and textbooks are more cost-effective than teacher training. Academic education more cost-effective than vocational.
Heyneman and Loxley (1983)	Examined the influence of family background and school factors on pupils' science achievement scores in 16 developing and 13 developed countries Mostly IEA data base	Found larger effect of school factors in lower-income countries than in high-income countries.
Armitage, et al. (1986)	Longitudinal survey of 4900 students over 2 years in NE Brazil	Teacher quality and instructional materials have significant rural effect on pupil achievement but school building quality does not.
Thias and Carnoy (1972)	School data in Kenya (1968) on costs, boarding, class size and average student score on national exam	School costs significant in contributing to achievement at secondary but not primary level. Whether students board at school and teacher experience also significant.
Fuller and Chantanavich (1976)	27 thousand primary school students in Thailand data	Significant but small effect of teacher education on pupil and school achievement. Teacher expectations also have significant effect.
Schiefelbein and Farrell (1973)	Pupil data in Chile (primary and secondary schools), individual achievement and school inputs	School materials contribute to student achievement but not teacher education. Increased focus on homework has positive effect.

Table 25 (cont.). Improving the Quality of Education: Selected Empirical Studies in Developing Countries

Study	Data Base	Results
Carnoy (1971)	School data on one-third of all public school students in Puerto Rico (1968)	Significant effect of teacher quality on low-income pupils' achievement at primary level. Length of school day significant.
Haron (1977)	89 secondary schools in Western Malaysia, more than 7,000 pupils	Length of teacher training significant in explaining student achievement. Class size not significant.
Carnoy and Thias (1977)	Four thousand pupils in 16 Tunisian secondary schools	Teacher quality not significant in explaining value added to student achievement (achievement relative to national final primary school exam). Boarding has positive effect on value added.
Loxley (1984)	Survey of 869 students in 37 schools in Botswana	School effects on reading and math achievement greater than family characteristics. Teacher training and library resources particularly important.

Table 26. Education and Technology: Selected Empirical Studies in Developing Countries

Study	Data Base	Results
Radio and Education		
Hall and Dodds (1977)	Review of three radio campaigns in Tanzania during 1969-1971.	Was useful in inculcating community health habits, awareness of voting rights, etc.
Cassirer (1977)	Senegal's UNESCO-financed pilot radio project.	Facilitated dialogue between peanut farmers and government.
Suppe, et al. (1978)	Nicaraguan radio mathematics project grades 1-4 mathematics courses in the region of Carazo and Rio San Juan provinces during 1975-1978.	Radio class pupils had better test scores than those in control groups but attendance, dropout, and repetition were not affected.
Hudson, (1977)	Northern pilot project of Canada.	Increased flow of information inside and outside the communities. Increased awareness of regional interests and activities. Government bodies become more responsible to local demands.
Oxford, et al. (1986)	Kenya radio language arts project (1981-1984).	Helped elementary students perform better in listening and reading.
UNESCO (1976)	Radio project in Thailand.	Radio instruction had positive impact on music, dancing, and singing, but no positive effect on social studies.
Jamison and McAnany (1978)	Tarahumara radio schools: remote region in Chihuahua Mexico during 1957-1972 (did not continue after 1972).	Radio-instructed pupils performed better in Spanish and math.
Walker (1986)	Radio-assisted community-based education, Dominican Republic.	Low cost and cost-effective, relative to traditional education (preliminary findings).
White (1977)	Popular cultural action of Honduras: ACPH radio schools for peasants.	Literacy was not a priority for peasants. They preferred oral programs.
Spain, Jamison, and McAnany (1977)	Series of case studies.	Radio generally highly effective in achieving variety of educational objectives at low cost.

Table 26 (cont.). Education and Technology: Selected Empirical Studies in Developing Countries

Study	Data Base	Results
Anzalone (1987)	Review of studies on education and media.	Radio when properly used can be an effective way to improve student achievement in a variety of subjects. Also relatively cost-effective.

Television as an Educational Medium

Study	Data Base	Results
Schramm, et al. (1981)	American Samoa television-assisted instruction.	High $166/pupil/year cost. No significant effect on student performance after seven years. Resistance by teachers result of noninvolvement in planning.
Clearinghouse on development communication (1982)	The Niger experimental Teacher training program.	High $1156/pupil/year cost. Reduced dropouts from 40 percent to 4 percent.
Kaye (1976)	Ivory Coast. Started in 1971 (funded by World Bank, presently discontinued.)	$13/pupil/year. Improved spoken French. Maintenance a serious problem. Ultimately failed.
Mayo, et al. (1976)	El Salvador.	Expanded opportunity for secondary education. Cost: $26/student/year in 1972. The ETV students fared better than non-ETV students in 7th but not in 8th and 9th grades; in mathematics but not in sciences and social science (Mayo). Boys made larger achievement gains than girls.
Schramm (1967)	Colombia educational television.	$4/pupil/year. There was no significant performance gain by ETV students relative to non-ETV students except in grade 2 (language), grade 5 (math), and grade 4 (natural science).
Shukla (1979)	Satellite instructional TV experiment for disadvantaged children	Centralized programs did not address local cultural milieu. Program helped in pupils' language development.
Anzalone (1987)	Review of existing studies.	Use of television is expensive and contributes little to pupil achievement.

Table 26 (cont.) Education and Technology: Selected Empirical Studies in Developing Countries

Study	Data Base	Results
Computers and Education		
Carnoy, et al. (1986)	Review of available studies.	Developing countries are entering into computer literacy investment programs that are based more on nationalistic rhetoric than concrete cost-benefit analysis or even educational rationale. Main gains in programming skills in developed countries are usually made by students with computers at home.
Papagiannis (1987)	Review of existing studies.	Cost-effectiveness studies in the U.S. suggest that computers raise achievement, but are expensive relative to other media.
Becker (1987)	U.S. elementary schools.	About 77% of the time used in computers was for drill and practice in reading, language arts, and arithmetic. By 1985, five out of six primary schools had computers for instruction (an estimated 1 computer/40 pupils in 1987) and a majority of high schools had 15 or more computers for instruction.
Williams (1987)	Computers and gender gap. Trinidad and Tobago.	Within schools where computers were used in instruction, females had greater access than males, but outside of school, males had greater access.
Kulik, Kulik and Bangert-Drowns (1985)	Effects of computer-assisted instruction. A meta-analysis of 32 research studies.	Computer-assisted instruction has positive effect on the achievement of primary school students in various school subjects. Average effect size of 0.47 (considered high).
Levin, et al. (1984)	Pre- and posttest data on students in computer interventions in U.S. primary schools.	For a school with a fully equipped computer laboratory in the U.S., the cost would be $119/student/year (1980 estimate); hardware only a small fraction of total cost. Positive effect on pupil achievement, but less cost-effective than peer tutoring.
Freeman (1987)	Computer-classroom ethnography in one primary school in Grenada.	The use of computers is significantly disturbed by poor electrical supply.

Table 27. Improving Sector Management: Selected Empirical Studies in Developing Countries

Study	Data Base	Results
Fuller (1987)	Several school quality studies that include management variables in models explaining pupil achievement	Headmaster education and experience appear to have significant positive effect on pupil achievement.
Heyneman and Loxley (1983)	Students in 60 Egyptian primary schools	Students perform better in schools with principals who had attended more training courses.
Sembiring and Livingstone (1981)	Students in 124 Indonesian secondary schools	Student achievement strongly associated with headmasters' salary and teaching experience.
Morales and Pinellsiles (1977)	Students in 53 primary and secondary schools in Bolivia	Signficant relationship between student achievement and headmaster post-secondary education.
Figueroa (1986)	In-class observations in 5 primary schools in Mexico City	Principals' management styles, curriculum, and classroom organization differ markedly between public and private schools.

Technology in Education

5.18 For this reason, partial cost-effectiveness studies of particular educational inputs have often yielded more interesting and directly applicable results. World Bank research has focused on low-cost inputs, such as textbooks (Heyneman, 1980) and radio (Spain, 1977; Jamison, 1978; see also, Block, 1985; Friend and Koslow, 1985; Ministry of Education of Ethiopia, 1987; a summary of instructional hardware applications in developing countries by Anzalone, 1987). These have shown relatively high effectiveness-cost ratios compared to traditional inputs -- particularly radio and textbooks (Lockheed and Hanushek, 1987). In the United States, similar studies comparing peer-tutoring, adult-tutoring, and computer-assisted instruction show that all three forms of augmenting traditional education show positive effects on student achievement, but that peer-tutoring is by far the most cost-effective (Levin, et al., 1984). A sample of available empirical research on educational technology is presented in Table 26, page 53.

5.19 The results of such research suggest that in many low-income countries facing an increasing knowledge gap, additional school inputs, such as textbooks and radio, and additional delivery methods such as peer tutoring and more effective curricula and teacher-student interaction, have to be considered seriously as a way to reduce that gap in the next decade. But we need to know more, particularly about more effective curricula and methods of delivering formal schooling and teacher training.

Sector Management

5.20 More recent studies suggest that school management may also be a high yield resource in improving student achievement. Until now, production function studies of schooling -- which should reveal how to use existing resources more effectively -- have focused on relating school inputs to pupil achievement. But many of those who have observed the schooling process in both developed and developing countries conclude that the most important factor governing how well pupils do in school is school management (Table 27, page 56), which, in many developing country rural schools, is often dependent on either a single teacher or a school principal, the curriculum which the teachers use, the availability of textbooks and other teaching aids (which often depend on the cleverness of the teacher in making use of available resources), the amount of effort that teachers are willing to expend, and the involvement of the community in making learning and academic achievement a community goal. Except for the availability of textbooks, none of these factors (which we can describe as the "process" of schooling) enters into school production estimates.

5.21   Management is singularly important in defining the "charter" (or standard of excellence) of the school (Figueroa, 1986) and the charter, in turn, is crucial in defining how well students are expected to do (Meyer, 1970). Levin (1980) argues that curriculum and other management decisions -- many of them highly centralized -- also define the way and the amount that teachers teach, as well as class size, which leaves relatively little autonomy for the non-innovative teacher. Figueroa claims that in Mexican public schools, the principal spends most of his or her time dealing with the Ministry rather than with problems in the school. Several studies have identified headmaster education and experience as important variables that affect pupils' achievement (see Table 25, page 51). Recent reports on schooling in the United States, such as *A Nation at Risk*, or Goodlad's *A Place called School*, have also focused on school management -- particularly on principals, superintendents, and other school "leaders" and innovators.

5.22   We know that well-managed, effective schools share several characteristics: they display an orderly environment, emphasize academic achievement, set high expectations for student achievement, and are run by teachers or principals who expend an enormous amount of effort to produce effective teaching and encourage pupils to learn, no matter what their family background or gender. Few schools in developing countries display these features. But we know little about why that is the case or what steps to take to provide greater and more effective effort. Particularly in low-income countries, these steps should be based on low-cost strategies.

5.23   The World Bank's Education and Employment Division in the Population and Human Resources Department (PHR) is now undertaking a case study approach of effective schools in low-income and middle-income countries. This will go far in providing further information. A more careful analysis of low-cost, effective approaches to formal education, especially those that involve parents and the community and new kinds of curriculum, teacher training, and educational management, could yield important new evidence that could improve learning in low-income countries and regions.

5.24   In addition to such case studies, further information could be derived from a review of educational management studies. Many of these studies propose management models for education, or focus on the use of technology for better educational management at the ministerial planning level. The World Bank's focus in recent years has implicitly been on management models that tend to centralize control over curriculum and quality through educational media (especially radio); that is, such models implicitly attempt to make the learning process "teacher proof" as they simultaneously attempt to keep costs of improved quality low. But what is needed is an analysis of management models that work at the school level, especially in primary schools, to test if such alternatives could be even more effective than educational media or make the use of educational media and other inputs (textbooks, for example) more effective.

Science Education

5.25   The current changes in the world economy suggest that a strong preparation in science and mathematics education will be increasingly indispensable to improved productivity and economic development, as well as opening new possibilities for families to raise the quality of their everyday life. There is no evidence for this assertion beyond the higher salaries earned by those who specialize in scientific and technical fields. But, intuitively, it seems likely that the problem-solving approach to life and work situations that is conveyed by science and math education (when it is taught well) should serve economic and social development goals particularly well.

5.26   Low achievement in science and math and unfamiliarity with basic technical concepts are critical weaknesses throughout the developing world. This particularly hurts the ability of countries to absorb new technologies that help increase productivity. It also hurts countries in developing their own appropriate innovations to solve production problems on a day-to-day basis.

5.27   There are a number of different approaches to the teaching of science and math, and we need to know more about the pluses and minuses of such approaches. For example, there is a long-running debate in the developing countries about what (and therefore how) science and math should be taught and learned (King, 1985). Those who focus on a more traditional scientific curriculum argue that the principal reason for low science and math achievement in low-income countries is that there is a dire shortage of qualified science and math teachers. If that is the case, it may be possible to overcome the shortage by applying new technologies that provide opportunities for self-study to large numbers of students outside and within the traditional educational system. In the industrialized countries, it is being argued that computers in the classroom can and will greatly increase the efficiency of science and math instruction (U.S. Congress, Office of Technology Assessment, 1988; Raizen, 1988). Pilot programs in developing countries have demonstrated convincingly that traditional "low-tech" technologies such as radio can also enrich and improve instruction in math as well as in language, once the basic conditions for orderly teaching and learning have been established (Suppe, et. al., 1978).

5.28   But others contend that the main reason for low achievement is not the lack of adequately skilled teachers, but the inappropriateness and inefficiency of a curriculum that requires scientific knowledge and practice far from any local experience (see King, 1985). The science and math curriculum is imported. It does not take advantage of a great deal of scientific knowledge and mathematics capability in local communities. In addition, the science and math problems posed to pupils have little to do with local applications. Science and math is often not taught through problem-solving at all, but through rote memorization.

5.29   This debate can be documented with a review of literature and case studies. What is needed is a better foundation for understanding what assumptions lie behind many of the assertions and what evidence there is for the effectiveness of alternative approaches to improving science and math education in different development situations. We need to learn from UNESCO's experience in this field. And more information is needed about the spectacular student math and science results achieved by countries such as Japan, Hong Kong, and the Republic of Korea.

Higher Education, Scientific Research and Development, and Technology Transfer

5.30   Intuitively, it would seem that those countries with a greater number of scientists and engineers -- especially if they are involved in research and development -- have a much greater possibility of adapting and developing new technologies (Rosenberg, 1982; Bianchi, Carnoy, and Castells, 1988). There has been great concern in the United States, for example, that poor science and mathematics preparation on a broad scale in public school will handicap the United States' economic development relative to its principal competitors in the future (National Science Foundation, 1980; U.S. House of Representatives, 1983).

5.31   Because they are leaders in scientific innovation and their economic development depends on translating this innovation into higher productivity and new products, the industrialized countries are especially concerned with the relationship between higher education (training), scientific research, and the application of research results and training to the production of goods and services (technological diffusion). For these countries, finding the most effective model for building research capacity and high level training and linking them for commercial applications has a potentially enormously high payoff in increased economic growth. The NICs, some middle-income countries, and the larger low-income countries, such as India and China, which already have a significant scientific base, are also concerned about expanding their research capacity and translating it into more efficient and innovative production of goods and services for domestic consumption and especially for export. Finding the proper role for university-level training and research is fundamental to transforming these countries' production processes. At the same time, most low-income countries need to develop the scientific personnel who will understand fully the latest technological advances coming out of the industrialized countries and be able to adapt and apply them for local production of goods and services. These countries must therefore also be concerned about delivering high-quality university education -- even for a relatively small number of youth -- and its relationship to research and development, especially for the packaging of new (and old) technologies for local applications.

5.32   Cross-section and case studies provide convincing evidence that access to knowledge and technology, as well as social and political factors, are crucial to technological diffusion (Edquist, 1985; Edquist and Jacobsson, 1988). An important element in access to knowledge and technology is education. But understanding the nature of the relationship between education -- particularly higher education -- and technology transfer requires more information and evidence. Some will emerge from the present review of research on higher education by PHR's Education and Employment Division. More can be found through an analysis of case study research on technology transfer in developing countries (see, for example, Bianchi, Carnoy, and Castells, 1988).

5.33   The important issue in both reviews is the role of university technical and scientific education in technological diffusion, and whether there are mediating factors in converting high-level scientific and technical skills into increased productivity through new technology. These mediating factors could include the nature of university science, math and engineering curriculum (problem solving versus memorization), the link between university and industry (practical applications), the link between training programs and research and development, or the general economic, social and political conditions for innovation and innovative applications. The case of the Soviet Union stands out as one in which a massive program in scientific and technical education has not translated into rapid and widespread technological diffusion. Japan and the Republic of Korea are counter-examples.

5.34   One of the clearest indications of the gap in developing nations' capability of moving into the age of information technology is the relatively small fraction of the labor force with scientific and engineering education and the even smaller relative fraction of scientists and engineers involved in research and development in those countries.

5.35   Table 28, page 62, shows the enormous variation in the ratio of scientists and engineers (and technicians) per 1,000 of economically active population, as well as the high concentration of scientific and engineering manpower in high-income, technologically-advanced economies. More than 80 percent of all research and development manpower is found in five countries. And the countries that have shown the greatest advances in technology creation and adoption in recent years are those with the highest ratios of scientists and engineers. Nevertheless, the example of the Soviet Union, with its large scientifically and technically trained labor force but relatively inefficient and technologically backward manufacturing and services, indicates that scientific education alone is not enough to produce highly diffused technological change.

5.36   Although this is "circumstantial" evidence of the importance of science and technical education as a necessary, if not sufficient condition, for the diffusion of technology, it does suggest that future educational policy for economic development will focus much more on the capability of the educational system to produce highly qualified scientists, engineers, and technicians, as well as the private and public managers who can work with them in applying technology to production and services. In addition, there will be a greater focus on creating a "scientific outlook" in the broad base of developing societies. This implies that the quantity and quality of science and mathematics education (as measured in terms of what children learn) -- from the basic to university levels has taken on increased importance as the world economy shifts to information technology.

5.37   Another issue is whether the key elements of appropriate and efficient university education and its linkages to industry and research can be reproduced through lower-cost forms of higher education in order to achieve a similar impact on technology diffusion and increased productivity. Most of the research on "distance education," for example, has focused on its cost-effectiveness (Perraton, 1982) and the mechanics of using of technology in providing such distance education (Asian Development Bank, 1986). But what are the possibilities of distance education in increasing technological diffusion and innovation? Can the key elements of effective scientific and technical education for technology transfer be reproduced through non-traditional, lower-cost forms of higher education?

Educational Finance Reform

5.38   The present distribution of public expenditures on education is highly unequal. The relatively few individuals who gain access to higher education receive more subsidies (in absolute terms) than those at the lower levels (World Bank, 1986; Jallade, 1973; Jallade, 1974; Mingat and Tan, 1986). Jallade's early research in Colombia and Brazil showed that lower-income groups are taxed to subsidize higher-income groups' education, this primarily because of students' highly unequal social class distribution across different schooling levels and the much higher cost-per-student at higher levels of schooling. A more recent Bank study shows that even among students who finish secondary school and pass the entrance examination for university entry, those who actually enroll have lower test scores but much higher social class background than those who do not (Jimenez, 1986). This pattern of subsidies also exists within the university level in developed countries (Hansen and Weisbrod, 1969; Levin, 1987) and in developing countries (Yao Yao, 1987): lower social class students are more likely to attend lower cost, lower-esteemed universities when there exist within-country variations in university cost and "quality," and are likely to specialize in lower cost humanities faculties rather than high cost and high payoff engineering, law, or medicine.

5.39   Inequality in educational spending is substantially greater in the developing countries than in the developed (see World Bank, 1986, Table 11, reproduced here as Table 29, page 64) and greater in Sub-Saharan Africa than in Asia or Latin America. The higher the average level of schooling, the lower the inequality in spending. But developed countries and Latin American countries also tend to spend more per student on primary schooling than do Asian and Sub-Saharan Africa countries. Sub-Saharan Africa countries also have the highest ratio of university to primary cost-per-student. Furthermore, Latin America has drastically reduced spending per student at the secondary and especially the tertiary level relative to the primary level in the 1970s (Heller and Cheasty, 1984). These data do not account for differences in taxes paid by different groups, but, as Jallade shows, even accounting for higher taxes paid by higher-income groups, education generally provides a net transfer from lower-income to higher-income families.

5.40 As a response to high costs-per-student at the university level and this inequality in educational spending, the Bank has already produced a number of suggestions for financial reform (see Table 30, page 65). Studies have focused primarily on cost recovery (especially at the university level), reinvesting the recovered costs in lower levels of schooling to increase equity, and decentralizing education, particularly in order to encourage the mobilization of family resources through community contributions to public schools and the formation of private schools (World Bank, 1986).

5.41 Cost recovery schemes at the university level are appealing, particularly in Sub-Saharan Africa, where university spending-per-student may be 60 times as high as per primary school student, and there is a large excess demand for university places. Much of this cost in most Sub-Saharan Africa countries, furthermore, is in the form of student living allowances (World Bank, 1986). Eliminating student allowances and even charging tuition combined with student loan programs therefore seems a logical scheme to reduce public costs substantially and simultaneously reduce excess demand. The funds created by cost recovery could be reinvested in improving or expanding university education or in other levels of schooling -- the latter would be most efficient should the rate of return to lower levels of schooling be significantly higher than to university. Reinvestment in the primary level would achieve greater equity.

5.42 Critiques of university and secondary school cost recovery schemes have identified three principal problems: (1) The political problem -- they hit hardest at the politically vocal urban professional and middle classes. (2) The economic efficiency problem -- in many countries, the rate of return to investment in university and secondary education is high and higher than to the primary level. Further, even in those countries where the social rate of return does not justify large public investment in university education, future economic development may depend on an underlying infrastructure of highly trained scientists, engineers, and technicians. This would require selective cost recovery, focusing on students less economically valuable humanities, social sciences, and so forth. These are usually students from lower-income families. (3) The equity problem -- as Jimenez's work in Colombia (1986) suggests, even with a student loan program, lower-income students are less likely to attend university unless motivated with financial subsidies. A cost recovery scheme is therefore likely to reduce equity unless the public sector used recovered costs specifically to improve lower levels of schooling. There is no available evidence that such a shift has or would occur.

5.43 One reason that universities are especially expensive in Sub-Saharan Africa, aside from excessive living allowances, is that they are plagued by significant diseconomies of scale (Psacharopoulos, 1982). This suggests that there is considerable room for making universities more cost-effective by regionalizing certain expensive specialties and by developing alternatives to traditional, European-style university education (discussed below). The need to regionalize programs for lower-income, smaller countries is crucial if they hope to develop the creative and decisionmaking technical talent to adopt and modify high technology for local applications. The same is true for research and development programs. This requires more, not less, investment in higher education and research, but in a more cost-effective manner and one that probably transcends national boundaries.

5.44 Privatization is another appealing way to softening reduced public educational spending. It promises to mobilize private resources that would not be forthcoming in an entirely public system, because of the touted greater cost-effectiveness of private education (see, for

Table 28. Scientific and Technical Personnel by Level of Development

Country	Year	Econ. Active Pop. ('000)	R&D Sci. Total ('000)	R&D Sci. Techs. ('000)	R&D Sci. Sci./Eng. ('000)	Sci. & Tech. Potential Total ('000)	Sci. & Tech. Potential Tech. ('000)	Sci. & Tech. Potential Sci./Eng. ('000)
GROUP A: Primary Product, Low-Income								
Burundi	1961/1984	2,654	0.3	0.1	0.2	-	-	-
Nepal	1981/1981	10,518	0.4	0.1	0.3	11.0	7.3	3.7
GROUP B: Marginally Industrialized, Middle-Income								
El Salvador	1980/1980	1,622	1.6	-	-	7.3	1.8	5.5
Guatemala	1985/1984	2,254	2.7	-	-	12.7	7.1	5.6
Pakistan	1984-5/1986	28,872	23.3	14.0	9.3	100.5	-	100.5
GROUP C: Industrializing, Middle-Income, High Education								
Costa Rica	1985/1982	887	0.4	-	0.4	-	-	-
Cuba	1986/1985	3,540	19.5	9.2	10.3	139.5	-	139.5
Egypt	1983/1982	13,842	26.6	6.7	19.9	492.5	-	492.5
Indonesia	1985/1984	63,826	29.0	4.1	24.9	2,104.8	1,911.5	193.3
Peru	1981/1981	5,314	4.9	-	4.9	1,689.8	1,398.0	291.8
Sri Lanka	1985/1983	5,972	3.3	1.4	1.9	18.5	11.0	7.5
Zimbabwe	1982/1982	2,484	0.9	-	-	-	-	-
GROUP C-1								
China	1982/1982	524,907	27.0	-	-	7,466.0	-	-
India	1981/1982	244,605	93.7	-	-	1,949.0	-	-
GROUP D: Oil Exporters, Upper-Middle and High-Income								
Iran, Isl. Rep.	1982/1982	6,418	5.1	1.9	3.2	465.5	170.9	294.6
Nigeria	1983/1977	29,453	3.5	1.3	2.2	133.8	111.7	22.1
Venezuela	1986/1983	6,107	7.3	2.7	4.6	1,881.0	1,534.0	347.0
GROUP E: Newly Industrialized								
Argentina	1985/1982	11,452	10.5	-	10.5	2,232.1	1,696.4	535.7
Brazil	1985/1982	55,098	32.5	-	32.5	4,436.6	3,074.4	1,362.2
Chile	1985/1984	4,236	1.7	0.1	1.6	69.9	-	69.9
Cyprus	1985/1984	249	0.2	0.1	0.1	-	-	-
Greece	1983/1983	3,892	3.5	1.1	2.4	1,602.1	1,272.6	329.5
Israel	1986/1986	1,472	53.7	14.0	39.7	146.1	63.8	82.3
Korea, Rep. of	1986/1983	16,116	51.6	19.5	32.1	2,025.6	1,931.5	94.2
Malaysia	1980/1980	4,260	2.7	-	-	-	-	26.0
Mexico	1980/1984	22,066	46.6	29.5	16.7	-	-	-
Singapore	1986/1984	1,229	3.8	1.4	2.4	64.2	25.9	38.3
Yugoslavia	1981/1981	9,359	38.7	13.8	24.9	3,986.0	3,584.0	402.0
GROUP F: Industrialized								
Australia	1986/1981	7,481	36.2	12.0	24.2	2,093.0	1,709.6	383.4
Austria	1986/1981	3,388	12.8	6.1	6.7	153.9	-	153.9
Canada	1986/1984	12,870	57.1	20.6	36.5	7,042.6	5,802.1	1,240.4
Denmark	1985/1983	2,753	17.8	10.3	7.5	323.7	240.2	83.5
Finland	1985/1985	2,598	23.6	-	-	1,616.6	1,444.4	172.2
France	1985/1979	24,085	230.9	157.9	72.9	1,251.6	-	1,251.6
FRG	1985/1983	29,012	252.7	119.6	133.1	8,374.0	2,278.0	6,096.0
Italy	1986/1983	23,617	91.7	28.7	63.0	4,703.4	3,527.9	1,175.4
Japan	1985/1984	60,391	628.7	97.1	531.6	37,050.0	30,004.0	7,046.0
New Zealand	1981/1981	1,332	8.1	-	-	139.5	92.3	47.2
Spain	1986/1984	13,781	21.5	6.2	15.3	4,634.8	3,482.8	1,152.0
Switzerland	1985/1983	3,201	13.4	-	-	348.2	-	348.2
United States	1986/1983	119,540	728.6	-	728.6	3,431.8	-	3,431.8
USSR	1986	185,526	1,463.8	-	1,463.8	31,628.0	18,141.0	13,487.0

Education and Development: Evidence for New Priorities

R & D Sci. Per 1,000 Eco-Active Pop.			Potential Sci./Tech. Manpower Per 1,000 Eco-Active Pop.		
Total ('000)	Tech. ('000)	Sci./Eng. ('000)	Total ('000)	Tech. ('000)	Sci./Eng. ('000)
0.1	0.0	0.1	-	-	-
0.0	0.0	0.0	1.1	0.7	0.4
1.0	-	-	4.5	-	-
1.2	-	-	5.7	3.2	2.5
0.8	0.5	0.3	3.5	-	-
0.5	-	0.5	-	-	-
5.5	2.6	2.9	39.4	-	39.4
1.9	0.5	1.4	35.6	-	35.6
0.5	0.1	0.4	33.0	30.0	3.0
0.9	-	0.9	318.0	263.1	54.9
0.5	0.2	0.3	2.0	1.8	0.2
0.4	-	-	-	-	-
0.1	-	-	14.2	-	-
0.4	-	-	8.0	-	-
0.8	0.3	0.5	72.5	26.6	45.9
0.1	0.0	0.1	4.6	3.8	0.8
1.1	0.4	0.7	308.0	251.2	56.8
0.9	-	0.9	194.8	148.1	46.7
0.9	-	0.6	80.5	55.8	24.7
0.4	0.0	0.4	16.5	-	16.5
0.5	0.3	0.2	-	-	-
0.9	0.3	0.6	411.7	327.0	84.7
36.5	9.5	27.0	99.4	43.4	56.0
3.2	1.2	2.0	125.7	119.8	5.9
0.6	-	-	6.1	-	-
2.1	1.3	0.8	-	-	-
3.1	1.1	2.0	52.3	14.1	38.2
4.2	1.5	2.7	426.0	383.0	43.0
4.8	1.6	3.2	279.7	228.5	51.2
3.8	1.8	1.9	45.4	-	45.4
4.4	1.6	2.8	547.1	450.8	96.3
6.5	3.7	2.7	117.7	87.3	30.4
9.1	-	-	622.3	556.0	66.3
9.6	6.6	3.0	52.0	-	52.0
8.7	4.1	4.6	288.6	78.5	210.1
3.9	1.2	2.7	199.2	149.4	49.8
10.4	1.6	8.8	613.5	496.8	116.7
6.1	-	-	104.8	69.3	35.5
1.5	0.4	1.1	336.3	252.7	83.6
4.2	-	-	108.8	-	108.8
6.1	-	6.1	28.7	-	28.7
7.9	-	7.9	170.7	97.8	72.9

Table 29. Share of Cumulative Public Educational Expenditure
Appropriated by Various Socioeconomic Groups, 1980

Region	Percentage in the population (1)			Percentage of educational expenditure appropriated (2)			Appropriation ratio (2)/(1)		
	Rural workers	Manual workers	White-collar	Rural workers	Manual workers	White-collar	Rural workers	Manual workers	White-collar
Anglophone Africa	76	18	6	56	21	26	0.73	1.19	3.78
Francophone Africa	76	18	6	44	21	35	0.58	1.15	5.93
Asia	58	32	10	34	38	28	0.59	1.19	2.79
Latin America	36	49	15	18	51	31	0.49	1.04	2.03
Middle East and Africa	42	48	10	25	46	29	0.60	0.35	2.87
Developing countries	58	33	9	36	35	29	0.60	0.98	3.48
Developed countries	12	53	35	11	46	43	0.95	0.87	1.20

[a] The number of countries included in each region is given in appendix table 14.

Source: World Bank, 1986, *Financing Education in Developing Countries.*

example, Psacharopoulos, 1987; Jimenez, 1986; Jimenez, Lockheed and Wattanawaha, 1988), and because increased competition between private and public schools may make public schools more efficient.

5.45 A number of developing countries -- for example, the Republic of Korea, the Philippines, Thailand, Brazil, and Kenya -- have highly developed private systems of education catering to students from both high-income and low-income families. There is no question that private education mobilizes additional family resources, but little evidence that this promotes the public sector to invest the additional resources made available in more or better public schooling or that public schooling becomes more efficient as a result. Increasing the private costs of education through privatization (even through increasing school fees) may also reduce female enrollment, particularly where families value female education less than male education (Smock, 1981).

5.46 In Brazil, a private university system subsidized by the state was allowed to expand in the 1970s to absorb excess demand, especially from lower academically able (and lower-income) secondary graduates. These "diploma mills" absorbed excess demand by "taxing" lower-income families to take bank loans and pay tuition, while higher-income families continued to send their children to excellent public universities. Neither did the Brazilian government plow the resources released into a rapid expansion or increased quality of lower schooling levels. Brazil continued to invest a relatively small percentage of its GDP in education.

5.47 Although there are many examples in which private education is more efficient than public in producing high academic achievement (Jimenez, 1986; Jimenez, Lockheed, and Wattanawaha, 1988), there are also serious questions about the general validity of many of these studies (Levin, 1987). Counter-examples also exist, notably the large system of

Table 30. Alternative Financing Approaches: Selected Empirical Studies of Cost Recovery and Private Education in Developing Countries

Study	Data Base	Results
Cost Recovery		
World Bank, *Financing Education in Developing Countries* (1986)	Survey of studies on cost recovery and impact of private education	Cost recovery and fee-based private education have small negative impact on attendance and could mobilize considerable family resources for education. Possible positive impact on equalizing distribution of school spending.
Mingat and Tan (1986)	Published data on university graduates earnings; university enrollment	Simulation of student loan repayment under various assumptions of completion rates and loan conditions suggests that with small loans, even in Africa, university student loan schemes would recoup part of public costs. In Asia and Latin America, a high percentage of costs could be recovered.
Woodhall (1983)	Secondary data on student loans, by country, world-wide	Student loans are available for funding university education in 30 countries; the programs appear to be successful.
Jimenez (1987)	Data from household surveys on spending for education	Estimated price and elasticities suggest that average rate of enrollment might not fall if fees increase, although different income groups may be affected differently.
Kulakow, Brace, and Morrill (1978)	Case studies of mobilizing community resources for education	School gardens can produce output that could offset school costs.
Gustafsson (1988)	Case studies of education with production in Botswana and Zimbabwe	Production by pupils in school production units not an important cost-factor.
Tan, et al. (1984)	Three thousand primary and secondary school students in Malawi	Estimated demand functions for education suggest that user fees will have small effect on enrollment, but larger for low-income families.
Private Education		
Schiefelbein (1985)	Students in private and public schools	Private school students achieved more academically in Chile in 1982 than those in state schools, even when differences in social class are taken into account.
Jimenez (1986)	Students in private and public schools in Bolivia and Paraguay; school costs	Private school students achieve more academically even though unit costs in private schools are lower than in state schools.

Table 30 (cont.). Alternative Financing Approaches: Selected Empirical Studies of Cost Recovery and Private Education in Developing Countries

Study	Data Base	Results
Jimenez, Lockheed, and Wattanawaha (1988)	Sample of four thousand 8th grade students and 99 math teachers in Thailand in private and public schools	Students in private schools perform significantly better than their public school counterparts and private schools are also more cost-effective.
Coleman, et al. (1982)	Survey of students in United States in public and private Catholic schools	Catholic schools are more effective than public schools in helping students acquire cognitive skills.
Psacharopoulos (1987)	Sample of six thousand Colombian and four thousand Tanzanian secondary public and private school students	Private school students in Colombia seem to do better in academic subjects, but results are mixed. In Tanzania, private school students do worse. Cost of private schooling is lower.

"Harambee" schools in Kenya (Armitage and Sabot, 1985), whose graduates score much lower on national examinations and do much worse in the labor market than public school graduates. But an additional and crucial issue is whether private schools can satisfy the underlying social (public) goals of public education (Levin, 1987), such as bringing students from widely varying backgrounds into a common national social experience called the public school. In the case where public secondary schools cater to higher income, better academically prepared students, it is true that privatizing education may make education as a whole more accessible and effective for the poor (this is in part the Jimenez, Lockheed, and Wattanawaha (1988) argument). But in the case where the better students tend to go to private schools, privatizing education could take the pressure off the Ministry of Education to improve public education, reducing access for low-income families.

6

Conclusion

Where More Work is Needed

6.1   This review suggests that there is a wealth of data from which to develop relevant policy approaches to education in the 1990s. The relation between education and economic development is well documented. More than enough information is available to analyze the changes that have taken place, worldwide and in countries at different levels of development, in school enrollments, retention, and school finance. The experiences of the lending institutions in educational assistance are also available in great detail. And a number of crucial educational policy areas, such as vocational versus academic curriculum, improving the efficiency of the schooling process, technology in education, and alternative forms of financing education, have been extensively studied empirically. These empirical studies provide a rich source of results for policy direction. We can already draw a number of conclusions for such new policy approaches.

Education and the Changing International Division of Labor

6.2   As new technologies and production processes transform the international economy, the future of world development and of individual nations' places in it hinge much more than even a generation ago on the capacity to acquire, transmit and apply knowledge to work and everyday life. The production of manufacturing and high-valued services no longer filter down "naturally" from high-income to low-income countries based on labor costs alone. Because of new goods, such as consumer electronics, and new processes, such as numerically-controlled machine tools and computer-assisted design and manufacturing (CAD-CAM), the location of manufacturing and high-value services depends increasingly on the producers' capacity to control quality and manage flexible, information-based systems. Comparative advantage is now a function of labor and management quality, as well as low wages.

6.3   There is already compelling evidence that a well-educated labor force is critical to the success of economic policies promoting international competitiveness and sustained development. And investments in education are not only central to economic growth, they also further the effectiveness of investments in family planning, health and nutrition.

6.4   There is compelling evidence as well that increasing access to education contributes positively to more equitable income distribution and to reducing poverty. In the words of Nobel Prize-winning economist, Theodore Schultz, "... the decisive factors of production in improving the welfare of poor people are the improvement in population quality and advances in knowledge." Private and social benefits from incremental outlays on education are highest in the poor countries, and, in those countries, are highest for outlays on expanding and improving basic education, precisely the level which targets the most disadvantaged groups. Basic education imparts essential knowledge. But it also develops crucial attitudes and values --

especially a sense of self-efficacy, or "can do" -- needed to adopt new methods and adjust to rapid change. Thus, the sustainability and long-term effectiveness of other programs that target disadvantaged groups -- such as those that address issues related to safe motherhood, population, women in development, and the alleviation of poverty -- also hinge on the quality of educational opportunities available to these groups. Of special importance is the education of girls who are often faced with socioeconomic and cultural obstacles that make attending school difficult for them.

6.5   Now, however, with the revolution in information, biological transformation and materials sciences, every country's educational system has become fundamental to its national production and the way it participates in this changing international economy. The new technologies and production methods offer enormous possibilities for increased agricultural and industrial output. But they depend much more than previous technologies and methods on well-trained, flexible labor; innovative, problem-solving management; and cadres of highly-trained scientists, engineers, and social scientists, including some with sophisticated research skills needed to understand fully developments at the frontiers of knowledge and to assess how such advances can be applied locally. As technical requirements increase, more and better education -- particularly good science and math education at all levels -- is needed to develop that all-important attitude of "can do," as well as to impart essential knowledge and skills that allow adaptability and flexibility in the ever-changing job environment. More than ever, an educated population is needed to develop and apply emerging technologies appropriately to meet local development needs.

6.6   This is a challenge that confronts all economies participating in the world system. Preparing for a future marked by increasingly rapid science-based change means developing human resources that can respond to change with the necessary information and decisionmaking capability.

The Knowledge Gap

6.7   Just when more and better education is needed, much of the world's population is being left behind. Future workers and parents in poor countries should be getting a greater understanding of their physical and social environment. They should be increasingly capable of using information to improve the quality of their lives. They should even be catching up to industrial-country workers in what they know and in getting the opportunity to use it. Some are catching up. But, on average, differences in the acquisition of such knowledge -- the "knowledge gap" -- appear to be increasing between wealthy and poor economies, and, in many places, between the wealthy and the poor within countries.

6.8   One way to get a grip on the knowledge gap and how it is changing is to look at school enrollment and school quality across countries and over time.

6.9   Both governments and international donor agencies have invested heavily in education during the last three decades, producing impressive expansions of enrollment throughout the developing world at all levels of education. Yet the enrollment gap between the lowest-income countries and other countries widened during 1980-85. In high-income and middle-income countries gross enrollment ratios were at or above 100 percent by 1985. In the lowest-income countries, the ratio at the primary level rose from 38 percent in 1960 to 65 percent in 1980, but remained almost constant after 1980. By 1985, 100 million school-age children in developing countries were not in school. About 70 percent of these were in the lowest-income countries, 45 percent in South Asia (India, Pakistan, and Bangladesh) and 30 percent in Sub-Saharan Africa. Most were in rural areas and about 60 percent were girls.

6.10   The enrollment gap between lower-income and higher-income countries is even more obvious at higher levels of education. In secondary education, gross enrollment rates increased most rapidly in the highest income countries, to 85 percent in 1985. This compared to 64 percent in upper middle-income countries, 41 percent in lower middle-income, and 19 percent in low-income countries. In 1960, the gap was considerably less than in 1985. At the tertiary/university level, the 1985 enrollment rates ranged from 32 percent in the high-income countries, to 17 percent in high middle-income countries, 13 percent in low middle-income countries, and 2 percent in low-income countries, indicating the vast difference in access to higher education in countries at different levels of development. In part, the differences in secondary and higher enrollment reflect rational investment decisions based on different production structures, the derived demand for skills, and the pay-off to various levels of education. But such differences also imply highly differentiated capacities to take advantage of knowledge-based product and process innovations in all economic sectors. Those innovations hold the key to long-term welfare.

6.11 The gap between low-income and middle- and upper-income countries is most ominous in female and rural education. Past growth in enrollments has benefitted girls as well as boys, and girls represented a relatively high 40 percent of total enrollment in primary school in low-income countries in 1984 (as compared to 49 percent in middle- and higher-income countries). But this proportion drops off much more quickly at secondary and tertiary levels in low-income than in higher-income countries. This pattern is similar for rural young people. The worst off are rural girls in low-income societies. This lack of female education in rural, low-income societies may be a principal manifestation and reproducer of underdevelopment.

6.12 In addition to rising differences in enrollment rates and attainment levels, the knowledge gap may also be increasing in terms of educational quality. In 1960, the OECD countries spent 14 times more per student than low-income developing countries eligible for IDA loans. By 1980, the industrial nations were spending 50 times more per student than low-income countries. To the extent that the amount and nature of purchased inputs to educational processes are reflected in learning outcomes, this trend is ominous.

6.13 In more direct fashion, several international studies, comparing and analyzing differences in student achievement across many countries, document what is perhaps the most serious problem facing schools in developing countries: the apparent difficulty of communities, families, and schools to create an environment in which students can learn effectively. The studies show that students from industrial and newly industrializing countries greatly outperform students from lower-income countries on standardized achievement tests in reading, mathematics and science.

6.14 Students in developing countries' schools are therefore not only getting fewer years of education but are learning less in each of those years than students in higher-income countries. This is partly reflected in high repetition rates in primary and secondary schools. But even those who go straight through their school years are learning less language skills, mathematics, and science in low-income and most middle-income countries than in the newly-industrialized developing countries (NICs) and the industrialized countries. Since these competencies are fundamental to self-efficacy and developing flexible skills in today's rapidly-changing, industrializing environments, poor quality schooling has serious implications for a country's future ability to compete economically.

6.15 This is not to imply that only low-income countries are having difficulties in science and math education. Although students in the United States, for example, have high levels of scientific knowledge compared to most, a recent study reports that a low 7 percent of 17-year-olds were adequately prepared for college science courses, down from 8.5 percent in 1977.

Nations Face a Variety of Educational Problems Demanding Different Strategies

6.16 As successful participation in the world economy becomes more knowledge-intensive, all nations face the challenge of improving their educational systems. To varying degrees, all societies: (i) need to bring their education up-to-date in transmitting knowledge and skills for dealing with the problems of the future; (ii) need to equalize access to high quality schooling; (iii) need to raise the level of math, language and science acquisition; (iv) need to improve the effectiveness of educational resources; (v) need to develop new approaches to schooling the disadvantaged; and (vi) need to develop mechanisms for the generation, acquisition, and application of appropriate knowledge.

6.17   But not all countries -- and not even all developing countries -- face the same educational problems. Different educational and financial strategies are therefore appropriate to these widely differing conditions.

6.18   The highly industrialized countries, such as Japan, the United States, Canada, and most Western European economies, have by and large achieved universal secondary education and send a significant percentage of young people through university. They devote a relatively high percentage of their GNP to education. Almost all these countries consider that in the new context of international competition, with its emphasis on scientific innovation and creative management, educational quality -- as measured by learning outcomes -- at all levels of schooling requires close attention. For example, the United States is very concerned that its science and math education in the lower grades is not as good as in other major industrial economies, with important future consequences for its leadership in high tech innovation. The education of the disadvantaged (e.g. immigrants, low-income groups) at all levels of schooling is important enough in some countries to be of major concern as well. But because they are leaders in scientific innovation and their economic development depends on translating this innovation into higher productivity and new products, the industrialized countries are especially concerned with the relationship between higher education (training), scientific research, and the application of research results and training to the production of goods and services (technological diffusion). For these countries, finding the most effective model for building research capacity and high level training and linking them for commercial applications has a potentially enormously high payoff in increased economic growth.

6.19   A number of newly-industrialized developing countries (NICs), such as Mexico, Taiwan, and the Republic of Korea, and high-income oil producers, such as Saudi Arabia and Venezuela, have been generally successful in expanding their educational systems consistent with their economic and social development needs. In part this has been the result of good fortune (large oil reserves) or good public management in successfully mobilizing overall investment for economic growth. Most Asian countries, for example, have not had the financial constraints caused by slow economic growth in the 1980s, as is now typical in Sub-Saharan Africa and Latin America. This educational expansion has also been the result of a strong commitment to education as a fundamental building block of the development process. These more rapidly developing economies -- like the developed countries -- are capable of mobilizing domestic resources to increase the quantity and quality of education and vocational training, but still need to make efficient and effective investments at all schooling levels and in vocational training programs in order to sustain growth and equalize access to knowledge. They need to develop strong scientific and technical education to consolidate and then improve their competitive position in a changing world economy. Some are beginning to innovate and therefore, like the highly industrialized countries, are concerned about linking university training to research and to local industrial and service applications. Many of these countries must also confront educational inequities, particularly in female education and the education of lower-income students. But they are meeting the needs of the population for basic education, literacy is high, and many are well on the way to achieving a highly skilled labor force.

6.20   Many middle-income countries (for example, Colombia, Peru, the Philippines, Thailand) and some large, low-income countries (China and, to a lesser extent, India, for example) have essentially achieved universal primary schooling and have rapidly increased secondary and university enrollment. By focusing on new technologies and increasing their telecommunications and computer infrastructure, they are trying to transform their industries to play a more advanced role in the newly emerging world division of labor. The most important educational problems of these industrializing, middle-income, "high" education countries revolve around improving the quality of primary education (especially reducing dropouts and increasing learning) and expanding and improving secondary and university education -- particularly making it relevant for high tech development. They must make important decisions regarding vocational versus academic education, the introduction of new kinds of scientific, mathematical, information technology and technology management programs into their secondary and university curricula, research and development funding for universities, and new linkages between universities and industry and agriculture.

6.21   Countries in a fourth group have some industries or have high value exports and could industrialize. These include most of the Central American countries, some Sub-Saharan Africa countries such as Côte d'Ivoire, Nigeria, and Botswana, for example, and countries such as Pakistan. They conceivably could fit into the world's new industrializing process if they can improve and expand their knowledge base and labor skills and begin to focus on appropriate technological strategies. They often face financial constraints, high dropout rates in primary schools, wide knowledge gaps within their societies (urban and rural, girls and boys), and rapidly increasing school-age populations. These countries are concerned with secondary and university educational reforms for the information revolution, but also have to focus on basic education for reduced fertility, better health care and nutrition, and higher agricultural productivity. They must make fundamental improvements in the quality of basic education and may, in many cases, have to develop improved delivery strategies at the primary level to achieve universality and higher quality.

6.22   A fifth set of countries is still primarily agricultural, grappling with providing basic education to their population. Many Sub-Saharan Africa countries fall into this category, as well as Afghanistan, Bangladesh, and Nepal. They face severe financial and human resource constraints in developing their educational systems. At the same time, the information and biotechnology revolutions are placing increased pressures on them to produce cadres of highly-trained scientific and management personnel, as well as the highly productive skilled and semi-skilled workers that will give them some chance of participating in the new world economic system. Their basic education must receive primary attention, with increased focus on highly efficient ways of delivering the necessary literacy, math and science skills to the mass of their rural populations, including involving more community resources in primary education and greatly improving the level of teaching and school management.

6.23   These low-income economies face a whole different set of educational problems, beginning with difficulties in providing minimal basic education for a rapidly growing primary school population, achieving universal literacy, and developing adequate skills to raise low standards of living in rural and urban areas. Lack of financial resources, growing school-age population, skill shortages, and the inefficient use of resources are all barriers to educational expansion. Annual per capita GDP growth in low-income countries (excluding India and China) dropped from 0.6 percent in 1965-80 to 0.4 percent in 1980-86; and in low middle-income countries, from 3.8 percent in 1965-80 to -0.8 percent in 1980-86, although there was considerable variation in the latter group. Low-income countries (excluding India and China) had reached a per capita income of only US$200 in 1986. They spent the lowest proportion of their GDP on education — and this proportion declined from a high of 3.3 percent in 1975 to less than 3 percent in the 1980s. In these countries, teaching and management skills are in very short supply, and funds for education are lacking. The very nature of these problems is different from those of education in higher-income countries.

6.24   New educational approaches are important for all countries but urgent for those facing severe financial constraints. Poorer countries are increasingly less able financially to catch up using wasteful, poorly managed educational delivery systems that have little linkage with the community they are supposed to serve. In such economies, where high quality educational resources are extremely scarce, teachers have to draw effectively on the surrounding community to create an active learning environment and a problem-solving approach to math and science. Teacher and school management training should incorporate such methods as part of their curriculum. New financial approaches are also more urgent, especially for higher-cost secondary and higher education. The low-income countries spend much more per university student, relative to GNP per capita, than the industrialized countries or the NICs.

6.25   At the same time, low-income countries (like middle-income countries and the NICs) need to develop the scientific personnel who will understand fully the latest technological advances coming out of the industrialized countries and be able to adapt and apply them for local production of goods and services. These countries must therefore also be concerned about delivering high-quality university education -- even for a relatively small number of youth -- and its relationship to research and development, especially for the packaging of new (and old) technologies for local applications.

Bibliography

Education and Economic Growth: General

Denison, E. *The Sources of Economic Growth in the United States and the Alternatives before the U.S.* New York: Committee of Economic Development, 1962.

Denison, E. *Why Growth Rates Differ: Post War Experience in Nine Western Countries.* Washington, D.C.: The Brookings Institution, 1967.

Schultz, T. "Investment in Human Capital." *American Economic Review.* (51), 1961.

Solow, R. "Technical Change and the Aggregate Production Function." *Review of Economics and Statistics.* (39), 1957.

Ward, F. Champion. (ed.). *Education and Development Reconsidered: The Bellagio Conference Papers.* New York: Praeger Publishers, 1974.

Education and Economic Growth: What the Bank Has Done

Anderson, C. *Social Selection in Education and Economic Development.* EDT Discussion Paper No. 82, Washington, D.C.: World Bank, 1987.

Cochrane, S. and World Bank, Population, Health and Nutrition Department. *The Effects of Development on Fertility: Education and Residence.* Washington, D.C.: World Bank, 1981.

Colclough, C. *Primary Education and Economic Development: A Review of the Evidence.* World Bank Staff Working Paper No. 399, Washington, D.C.: World Bank, 1980.

Habte, A. "Education and National Development." *Finance and Development.* 19(2), 1982.

Habte, A., G. Psacharopoulos and S. Heyneman. *Education and Development: Views from the World Bank.* Washington, D.C.: World Bank, 1983.

Heyneman, S. P. and D. White (eds.). *The Quality of Education and Economic Development.* Washington, D.C.: World Bank, 1986.

King, T. and R. Berry. *Education and Income: A Background Study for World Development Report, 1980.* Washington, D.C.: World Bank, 1980.

Lockheed, M., D. Jamison and L. Lau. "Farmer Education and Farm Efficiency: A Reply." *Economic Development and Cultural Change.* 35(3), 1987.

Psacharopoulos, G. and M. Woodhall. *Education and Development: Analysis of Investment Choices.* New York: Oxford University Press, 1985.

Simmons, J. *Education, Poverty, and Development.* Washington, D.C.: World Bank, 1974.

World Bank. *The Assault on World Poverty: Problems of Rural Development, Education and Health.* Baltimore: Johns Hopkins University Press, 1965.

World Bank. *Education Sector Policy.* Washington, D.C.: World Bank, 1980.

Education and Productivity: General

Carnoy, M., H. Daley and R. Hinojosa. "The Changing Position of Minorities and Women in the U. S. Labor Market Since 1959." Stanford University, 1988. (mimeo)

Fuller, W. "Education, Training and Worker Productivity: Study of Skilled Workers in Two Firms in South India." Ph.D. Thesis: Stanford University, 1970.

Godfrey, M. "Education, Training and Productivity: A Kenyan Case Study." *Comparative Education Review.* (21), 1977.

Min, W. "The Impact of Vocational Education on Productivity in the Specific Institutional Context of China: A Case Study." Ph.D. Thesis: Stanford University, 1987.

Pachico, D. and J. Ashby. "Investments in Human Capital and Farm Productivity: Some Evidence from Brazil." Study Prepared for Cornell University (processed), 1976.

Patrick, G.F. and Kehrberg, E.W. "Costs and Returns of Education in Five Agricultural Areas of Eastern Brazil." *American Journal of Agricultural Economics.* (55)2, 1973.

Sack, R., M. Carnoy and C. Lecaros. "Educacion y Desarrollo Rural en America Latina," in *Problemas del Financiamiento de la Educacion en America Latina.* Washington, D.C.: Banco Interramericano de Desarrollo, 1980.

Education and Productivity: What the Bank Has Done

Berry, A. "Education, Income, Productivity and Urban Poverty," in King, K. (ed.), *Education and Income.* Washington, D.C.: World Bank, 1980.

Chou, E. and L. Lau. *Farmer Ability and Farm Productivity: A Study of Farm Households in the Chiangmai Valley, Thailand 1972-1978.* EDT Discussion Paper No. 62, Washington, D.C.: World Bank, 1987.

Clark, D. *How Secondary School Graduates Perform in the Labor Market: A Study of Indonesia.* World Bank Staff Working Paper No. 615, Washington, D.C.: World Bank, 1983.

Cotlear, D. *Farmer Education and Farm Efficiency in Peru: The Role of Schooling, Extension Services and Migration.* EDT Discussion Paper No. 49, Washington, D.C.: World Bank, 1986.

Jamison, D. and L. Lau. *Farmer Education and Farm Efficiency.* Baltimore: Johns Hopkins University Press, 1982.

Jamison, D. and P. Moock. "Farmer Education and Farm Efficiency in Nepal: The Role of Schooling, Extension Services and Cognitive Skills." *World Development.* 12(1), 1984.

Jimenez, E. "Evaluacion Economica de la Capacitacion: Perspectivas de Investigacion del Banco Mundial." In *Capacitacion, Productividad e Ingresos Laborales. Conference Proceedings of the Regional Seminar on Training, Productivity and Labor Income, Mexico City, February 25-March 1, 1985.* Mexico, D.F.: Organization of American States, 1985.

Jimenez, E., B. Kugler and R. Horn. *An Economic Evaluation of a National Training System: Colombia's Servicio Nacional de Aprendizaje (SENA).* EDT Discussion Paper No. 24, Washington, D.C.: World Bank, 1986.

Knight, J.B. and R. Sabot. *Overview of Educational Expansion, Productivity and Inequality: A Comparative Analysis of the East African Natural Experiment.* EDT Discussion Paper No. 48, Washington, D.C.: World Bank, 1986.

Lockheed, M., D. Jamison and L. Lau. "Farmer Education and Farmer Efficiency: A Survey." *Economic Development and Cultural Change.* (29)1, 1980.

Lockheed, M., D. Jamison and L. Lau. "Farmer Education and Farm Efficiency: A Reply." *Economic Development and Cultural Change.* 35(3), 1987.

Metcalf, D. *The Economics of Vocational Training: Past Evidence and Future Considerations.* World Bank Staff Working Paper No. 713, Washington, D.C.: World Bank, 1985.

Perraton, H., D. Jamison and F. Orivel. *Basic Education and Agricultural Extension.* Baltimore: Johns Hopkins University Press, 1982.

Perraton, H., et. al. *Basic Education and Agricultural Extension: Costs, Effects, and Alternatives.* World Bank Staff Working Paper No. 564, Washington, D.C.: World Bank, 1983.

Psacharopoulos, G. and A. M. Arriagada. *The Educational Attainment of the Labor Force: An International Comparison.* EDT Discussion Paper No. 38, Washington, D.C.: World Bank, 1986.

Psacharopoulos, G., et. al. *Manpower Issues in Educational Investment: A Consideration of Planning Processes and Techniques.* World Bank Staff Working Paper No. 624, Washington, D.C.: World Bank, 1983.

World Bank. *World Development Report, 1980. Part II - Poverty and Human Development.* Washington, D.C.: World Bank, 1980.

World Bank. *Education in Sub-Saharan Africa: Policies for Adjustment, Revitalization, and Expansion.* Washington, D.C.: World Bank, 1987.

Benefit-Cost Analysis: General

Blaug, M. *An Introduction to the Economics of Education.* London: Penguin Press, 1970.

Carnoy, M., H. Daley and R. Hinojosa. *The Changing Economic Position of Minorities and Women in the U.S. Labor Market Since 1959.* Stanford University, Center for Chicano Studies, 1988 (mimeo).

Carnoy, M. and D. Marenbach. "The Return to Schooling in the U.S., 1939-69." *Journal of Human Resources.* (X)3, 1975.

Freeman, R. B. *The Overeducated American.* New York: Academic Press, 1976.

Patrick, G. and E. Kehrberg. "Costs and Returns of Education in Five Agricultural Areas of Eastern Brazil." *American Journal of Agricultural Economics.* (55)2, 1973.

Psacharopoulos, G. *Returns to Education: An International Comparison.* Amsterdam: Elsivier, 1973.

Ryoo, J. "Changes in Rates of Return Over Time: A Case of Korea." Ph.D. Thesis: Stanford University, 1988.

Benefit-Cost Analysis: What The Bank Has Done

Behrman, J. and Birdsall, N. *Three Studies in the Economics of Education Using Brazilian Data,* 1983.

Birdsall, N. and Behrman, J. *Income Returns to Quantity and Quality of Schooling in Brazil: Is Quantity Alone Misleading?* Population and Human Resources Division, Washington, D.C.: World Bank, 1982.

Bussink, W. *Poverty and the Development of Human Resources -- Regional Perspectives: A Background Paper for World Development Report, 1980.* Washington, D.C.: World Bank, 1980.

Clark, D. *How Secondary School Graduates Perform in the Labor Market: A Study of Indonesia,* World Bank Staff Working Paper No. 615, Washington, D.C.: World Bank, 1983.

Cochrane, S. *Fertility and Education: What Do We Really Know?* Baltimore: Johns Hopkins University Press, 1979.

Cochrane, S., D. O'Hara, and J. Leslie. *The Effects of Education on Health,* World Bank Staff Working Paper No. 405, Washington, D.C.: World Bank, 1980.

Grawe, R. *Ability in Pre-schoolers: Earnings and Home Environment,* World Bank Staff Working Paper No. 322, Washington, D.C.: World Bank, 1979.

Heyneman, S. *The Evaluation of Human Capital in Malawi.* World Bank Staff Working Paper No. 420, Washington, D.C.: World Bank, 1980.

Heyneman, S. and P. Mintz. *Investment in Indian Education, Uneconomic?* Baltimore: Johns Hopkins University Press, 1979.

Hicks, N. and J. Boroumand. *Economic Growth and Human Resources: A Background Paper for World Development Report, 1980.* Washington, D.C.: World Bank, 1980.

Hinchliffe, K. *The Monetary and Non-Monetary Returns to Education in Africa.* EDT Discussion Paper No. 46, Washington, D.C.: World Bank, 1986.

Horn, R. and E. Jimenez. *Does In-Service Training Affect Self-Employed Earnings? The Colombian Case.* EDT Discussion Paper No. 66, Washington, D.C.: World Bank, 1987.

Jallade, J. P. *Basic Education and Income Inequality in Brazil: The Long-Term View,* World Bank Staff Working Paper No. 268, Washington, D.C.: World Bank, 1977.

Jamison, D. and J. van der Gaag. *Education and Earnings in the People's Republic of China.* EDT Discussion Paper No. 56, Washington, D.C.: World Bank, 1987.

Jimenez, E. and B. Kugler. "The Earnings Impact of Training Duration in a Developing Country: An Ordered Probit Selection Model of Colombia's Servicio Nacional de Aprendizaje." *Journal of Human Resources.* 22(2), 1987.

Jimenez, E. and B. Kugler. *Does SENA Matter? Some Preliminary Results on the Impact of Colombia's National Training System on Earnings.* EDT Discussion Paper No. 2, Washington, D.C.: World Bank, 1985.

Knight, J. and R. Sabot. *The Returns to Education: Increasing with Experience or Decreasing with Expansion?* Population and Human Resources Division, Washington, D. C.: World Bank, 1981.

Mingat, A. and J. Tan. *The Economic Returns to Investment in Project-Related Training: Some Evidence from World Bank Projects.* EDT Discussion Paper No. 89, Washington, D.C.: World Bank, 1987.

Perraton, H. *Alternative Routes to Formal Education: Distance Teaching for School Equivalency,* Baltimore: Johns Hopkins University Press, 1982.

Psacharopoulos, G. *Higher Education in Developing Countries: A Cost Benefit Analysis.* World Bank Staff Working Paper No. 440, Washington, D.C.: World Bank, 1980.

Psacharopoulos, G. *Time Trends of the Returns to Education: Cross-National Evidence.* EDT Discussion Paper No. 94, Washington, D.C.: World Bank, 1987.

Psacharopoulos, G. "Returns to Education: A Further International Update and Implications." *Journal of Human Resources.* (20), 1985.

Psacharopoulos, G. *Higher Education in Developing Countries: A Cost-Benefit Analysis,* World Bank Staff Working Paper No. 440, Washington, D.C.: World Bank, 1980.

Psacharopoulos, G. and M. Woodhall. *Education and Development: Analysis of Investment Choices.* New York: Oxford University Press, 1985.

Psacharopoulos, G. and F. Steier. *Education and the Labor Market in Venezuela.* EDT Discussion Paper No. 93, Washington, D.C.: World Bank, 1987.

Psacharopoulos, G. "Returns to Education: An Updated International Comparison." *Comparative Education.* 17(3), 1981.

Simmons, J. *The Determinants of Earnings: Towards an Improved Model,* Washington, D.C.: World Bank, 1974.

Suarez-Berenguela, R. *Peru Informal Sector, Labor Markets, and Returns to Education.* LSMS Working Paper No. 32, Washington, D.C.: World Bank, 1987.

Thias, H. and M. Carnoy. *Cost-Benefit Analysis in Education: A Case Study of Kenya.* Baltimore: Johns Hopkins University Press, 1972.

Wheeler, D. *Human Resource Development and Economic Growth in Developing Countries: A Simultaneous Model.* World Bank Staff Working Paper No. 407, Washington, D.C.: World Bank, 1980.

Zymelman, M. *Occupational Structures of Industries.* Washington, D.C.: World Bank, 1982.

The Education of Women: General

Arriaga, E. and K. Davis. "The Pattern of Mortality Change in Latin America." *Demography.* 6(3), 1969.

Black, Naomi and B. Cottrells (eds.). *Women and World Change: Equity Issues in Development.* Beverly Hills: Sage, 1981.

Bowman, J. and A. Anderson. "The Participation of Women in Education in the Third World," in Kelly, G. and C. Elliott (eds.), *Women's Education in the Third World: Comparative Perspectives.* Albany: State University of New York Press, 1982.

Carnoy, M. "High Technology and International Labor Markets." *International Labor Review.* 124(6), 1985.

Christiansen, N. L., et. al. "Social Environment as it Relates to Malnutrition and Mental Development," in Cravioto, J., et. al., *Early Malnutrition and Mental Development.* Stockholm: The Swedish Nutrition Foundation, 1974.

Cravioto, J. and L. Delicardie. "Longitudinal Study of Language Development in Severely Malnourished Children," in Serban, G. (ed.), *Nutrition and Mental Function.* New York: Plenum Press, 1975.

Gans, B. "Some Socioeconomic and Cultural Factors in West African Pediatrics." *Archives of Disease in Childhood.* 38(197), 1963.

Graves, G. "Nutrition and Infant Behaviour: A Replication Study in the Kathmandu Valley, Nepal." *American Journal of Clinical Nutrition.* (31), 1978.

Haller, T. "Education and Rural Development in Colombia." Ph.D. Thesis: Purdue University, 1972.

Kelly, G. and C. Elliott. *Women's Education in the Third World: Comparative Perspectives.* Albany: State University of New York Press, 1982.

Kim, Y. "Education and Gender Inequality in Earnings in the Structured Labor Market: A Case Study of Korea." Ph.D. Thesis: Stanford University, 1987.

Levinson, F. *Morinda: An Economic Analysis of Malnutrition Among Young Children in Rural India.* Cambridge, Mass.: Cornell/MIT International Nutrition Policy Series, 1974.

Ryoo, J. "Changes in Rates of Return Over Time: A Case of Korea." Ph.D. Thesis: Stanford University, 1988.

Sivard, R. L. *Women... A World Survey.* Washington: World Priorities Group, 1985.

Smock, A. *Women's Education in Developing Countries: Opportunities and Outcomes.* New York: Praeger, 1981.

Strober, M. and H. Arnold. *Integrated Circuits/Segregated Labor: Women in Computer-related Occupations and High Tech Industries.* Stanford: CERAS, 1987.

Stromquist, N. *Determinants of Educational Participation and Achievement of Women in the Third World: A Review of Evidence and A Theoretical Critique.* Stanford: CERAS, 1988.

United Nations. *Relationships Between Fertility and Education: A Comparative Analysis of World Fertility Survey Data for 22 Developing Countries.* New York: U.N., 1983.

The Education of Women: What the Bank Has Done

Arriagada, A. M. "Occupational Training and the Employment and Wages of Peruvian Women." (forthcoming)

Birdsall, N. and B. Boulier. "The Effects of Family Planning Programs on Fertility in the Developing World," 1985.

Bulatao, R. *Reducing Fertility in Developing Countries: A Review of Determinants and Policy Levers.* World Bank Staff Working Paper No. 680, Washington, D.C.: World Bank, 1984.

Bulatao, R. and E. Bulatao. *Effects of In-School Population Education.* Technical Notes No. 86-18, Washington, D.C.: World Bank, 1986.

Castaneda, T. *Fertility, Child Schooling and Mothers' Labor Market Participation in Chile.* EDT Discussion Paper No. 34, Washington, D.C.: World Bank, 1986.

Castaneda, T. *The Determinants of Mothers' Labor Force Participation in Colombia.* EDT Discussion Paper No. 34, Washington, D.C.: World Bank, 1986.

Cochrane, S. "Effects of Education and Urbanization on Fertility," in *Determinants of Fertility: A Summary of the Knowledge.* Washington, D.C.: National Academy of Sciences, 1983.

Cochrane, S. "Women and Development Education and Fertility." *Finance and Development.* September 1988.

Cochrane, S. *The Effects of Education on Fertility and Mortality.* EDT Discussion Paper No. 26, Washington, D.C.: World Bank, 1986.

Cochrane, S. "Education and Fertility: An Expanded Examination of the Evidence." In Kelly, G. and C. Elliot (eds.), *Women's Education in the Third World: Comparative Perspectives.* Albany: State University of New York Press, 1982.

Cochrane, S. *Fertility and Education: What Do We Really Know?* Baltimore: Johns Hopkins University Press, 1979.

Cochrane, S. *The Effects of Education and Urbanization on Fertility,* EDT Discussion Paper No. 26, Washington, D.C.: World Bank, 1986.

Cochrane, S. and S. Farid. *Fertility in Sub-Saharan Africa: Levels and Their Explanation*, PHN Technical Note No. 85-13, Washington, D.C.: World Bank, 1986.

Cochrane, S., D. O'Hara, and J. Leslie. *The Effects of Education on Health*. Staff Working Paper No. 405, Washington, D.C.: World Bank, 1980.

Cochrane, S., J. Leslie, and D. O'Hara. "Parental Education and Child Health: Intra-Country Evidence." *Health Policy and Education*. (2), 1982.

Heaver, R. *Adapting the Training and Visit System for Family Planning, Health, and Nutrition Programs*. World Bank Staff Working Papers No. 662, Washington, D.C.: World Bank, 1984.

Herrera, M. and C. Super. *School Performance and Physical Growth of Underprivileged Children: Results of the Bogota Project at Seven Years*. PHN Technical Notes No. RES-8, Washington, D.C.: World Bank, 1983.

Horn, R. and A.M. Arriagada. *The Educational Attainment of the World's Population: Three Decades of Progress*. EDT Discussion Paper No. 37, Washington, D.C.: World Bank, 1986.

Hornik, R. *Nutrition Education: A State of the Art Review*, PHN Technical Notes No. RES-12, Washington, D.C.: World Bank, 1984.

Jamison, D. "Child Malnutrition and School Retardation in China." *Journal of Development Economics*. (20), 1986.

King, E. *Does Education Pay in the Labor Market? The Labor Force Participation, Occupation and Earnings of Peruvian Women*. LSMS Working Paper No. 67, Washington, D.C.: World Bank, 1989.

King, E. and A. M. Arriagada. "The Effect of Vocational and Technical Training on Women's Earnings and Employment in Developing Countries." (forthcoming)

King, E. and M. Shifferaw. "Vocational and Technical Training Opportunities for Women in Developing Countries." (forthcoming)

Mehta, T. "Population Education in Bank Projects" (Guidelines), 1981. (mimeo)

Middleton, J. and R. Lapham. "Demand Generation." in Lapham, R. and G. Simmons (eds.), *Organizing for Effective Family Planning Programs*. Washington: National Academy Press, 1987.

Moock, P. and J. Leslie. "Childhood Malnutrition and Schooling in the Terai Region of Nepal." *Journal of Development Economics*. (20), 1986.

Psacharopoulos, G. and M. Woodhall. *Education and Development: Analysis of Investment Choices*. New York: Oxford University Press, 1985.

Psacharopoulos, G. and Z. Tzannatos. *Female Labor Force Participation and Education*, The World Bank Research Observer, 3(2), 1989.

Selowsky, M. Nutrition, "Health and Education: The Economic Significance of Complementarities at Early Age," World Bank Reprint Series No. 218, Washington, D.C.: World Bank, 1981.

Stromquist, N. *School-Related Determinants of Female Primary School Participation and Achievement in Developing Countries: An Annotated Bibliography.* EDT Discussion Paper No. 83, Washington, D.C.: World Bank, 1987.

Tan, J. P. and M. Haines. *Schooling and Demand for Children: Historical Perspectives.* World Bank Staff Working Paper No. 697, Washington, D.C.: World Bank, 1984.

Young, M. *The Barefoot Doctor: Training, Role and Future,* PHN Technical Notes No. 405, Washington, D.C.: World Bank, 1984.

Zachariah, K. C. and S. Patel. *Determinants of Fertility Decline in India.* World Bank Staff Working Paper No. 699, Washington, D.C.: World Bank, 1984.

Education and Poverty: General

Carnoy, M., H. Daley and R. Hinojosa. "The Changing Economic Position of Minorities and Women in the U.S. Labor Market Since 1959." Stanford University, Center for Chicano Studies, 1988 (mimeo).

Carnoy, M., et. al. *Can Education Equalize Income Distribution in Latin America?* Geneva: ILO, 1978.

Chiswick, B. and J. Mincer. "Time Series Changes in Personal Income Inequality in the United States from 1939 to 1985." *Journal of Political Economy.* (80), 1972.

Langoni, C. "Income Distribution and Economic Development in Brazil." *Conjuntura Economica.* (27), 1973.

Leonor, M. and P. Richards. *Education and Income Distribution in Asia.* An ILO-WEP Study. London: Crom Helm, 1980.

Moynihan, D. *The Negro Family.* Cambridge, Mass.: MIT Press, 1967.

Ribich, T. *Education and Poverty.* Washington: The Brookings Institution, 1968.

Smith, J. and F. Welch. *Closing the Gap.* Santa Monica, CA: Rand Corporation, 1986.

Sowell, T. *Markets and Minorities.* New York: Basic Books, 1977.

Thurow, L. *Poverty and Discrimination.* Washington, D.C.: The Brookings Institution, 1970.

Education and Poverty: What the Bank Has Done

Birdsall, N. and O. Meesook. *Child Schooling, Number of Children and the Intergenerational Transmission of Inequality: A Simulation.* Washington, D.C.: World Bank, 1981.

Bowman, M. *Education and Income.* World Bank Staff Working Paper No. 401, Washington, D.C.: World Bank, 1980.

Dougherty, C. and E. Jimenez. *The Specification of Earnings Functions: Tests and Implications.* EDT Discussion Paper No. 100, Washington, D.C.: World Bank, 1987.

Jamison, D. and J. van der Gaag. *Education and Earnings in the People's Republic of China.* EDT Discussion Paper No. 56, Washington, D.C.: World Bank, 1987.

Jimenez, E. and Tan, J. *Selecting the Brightest for Post Secondary Education in Columbia: The Impact on Equity,* 1987.

Knight, J. and Sabot, R. *Educational Expansion and the Kuznets Effect,* Dec. 1983.

Komenan, A. *Education, Experience Et Salaires En Cote d'Ivoire: Une Analyse a Partir de l'Enquete de Main d'Oeuvre de 1984.* EDT Discussion Paper No. 99, Washington, D.C.: World Bank, 1987.

Meerman, J. *The Distribution of Public Expenditure for Education and Agriculture in Malaysia: Methodological Issues and a New Approach.* Washington, D.C.: World Bank, 1977.

Psacharopoulos, G., A. M. Arriagada, and E. Velez. *Earnings and Education Among the Self-Employed in Colombia.* EDT Working Paper No. 70, Washington, D.C.: World Bank, 1987.

Sabot, R.H. *Does the Expansion of Education Compress the Structure of Wages and Reduce the Inequality of Pay?: A Preliminary Analysis.* Washington, D.C.: World Bank, 1981.

World Bank. *Wage Determinants and School Attainment Among Men in Peru.* LSMS Working Paper No. 38, Washington, D.C.: World Bank, 1988.

World Bank. *Child Schooling and the Measurement of Living Standards.* LSMS Working Paper No. 14, Washington, D.C.: World Bank, 1982.

World Bank. *The World Bank's Support for the Alleviation of Poverty.* Washington, D.C.: World Bank, 1988.

World Bank. *Focus on Poverty.* Washington, D.C.: World Bank, 1983.

The Educational Spending Crisis: General

Heller, P. S. and A. Cheasty. "Sectoral Adjustment in Government Expenditure in the 1970s: The Education Sector in Latin America." *World Development.* (12), 1984.

Carnoy, M. "Educational Reform and Planning in the Current Economic Crisis." *Prospects* (16)2, 1986.

The Educational Spending Crisis: What the Bank Has Done

Arriagada, A. M. "Comparative Educational Policies in 12 Sub-Saharan African Countries," February, 1986 (mimeo).

Castaneda, T. *Innovations in the Financing of Education: The Case of Chile.* EDT Discussion Paper No. 35, Washington, D.C.: World Bank, 1986.

Eicher, J. C. *Educational Costing and Financing in Developing Countries: Focus on Sub-Saharan Africa.* World Bank Staff Working Paper No. 655, Washington, D.C.: World Bank, 1984.

Haddad, W. and T. Demsky. *Planning and Mobilization of Financial Resources for Education in the Middle East.* EDT Discussion Paper No. 92, Washington, D.C.: World Bank, 1987.

Hinchliffe, K. *Federal Finance, Fiscal Imbalance and Educational Inequality.* EDT Discussion Paper No. 72, Washington, D.C.: World Bank, 1987.

Komenan, A. and C. Grootaert. *Teachers/Non-Teachers Pay Differences in Côte d'Ivoire.* PPR Working Paper No. 12, Washington, D.C.: World Bank, 1988.

Mingat, A. and G. Psacharopoulos. *Education Costs and Financing in Africa: Some Facts and Possible Lines of Action.* EDT Discussion Paper No. 13, Washington, D.C.: World Bank, 1985.

Moock, P. *Education in Malaysia: A Review of Expenditures and Discussion of Issues.* EDT Discussion Paper No. 11, Washington, D.C.: World Bank, 1985.

Psacharopoulos, G., J. P. Tan and E. Jimenez. *The Financing of Education in Latin America: Issues and Lines of Action.* EDT Discussion Paper No. 32, Washington, D.C.: World Bank, 1986.

Psacharopoulos, G. *Are Teachers Overpaid? Some Evidence from Brazil.* EDT Discussion Paper No. 95, Washington, D.C.: World Bank, 1987.

Schiefelbein, E. *Education Costs and Financing Policies in Latin America.* EDT Discussion Paper No. 60, Washington, D.C.: World Bank, 1987.

Schultz, P. "Education Investment and Returns in Economic Development," Feb. 1986. (mimeo)

Tan, J. P. "The Private Direct Cost of Secondary Schooling in Tanzania," March 1984. (mimeo)

Wolff, L. *Controlling the Costs of Education in Eastern Africa: A Review of Data, Issues, and Policies.* World Bank Staff Working Paper No. 702, Washington, D.C.: World Bank, 1984.

World Bank. *Financing Education in Developing Countries: An Exploration of Policy Options.* Washington, D.C., 1986

Vocational and Academic Secondary Education: General

Arriagazzi, L. "Chile: Evaluating the Expansion of A Vocational Training Program," in Coombs, P.H. and J. Hallak (eds.), *Educational Cost-analysis in Action: Case Studies for Planners, Vol. I.* Paris: UNESCO, IIEP, 1972.

Bacchus, K. "The Political Context of Vocationalisation of Education in the Developing Countries," in Lauglo, and Lillis (eds.), *Vocationalising Education.* London: Pergamon Press, 1988.

Borus, M. "A Cost-Effectiveness Comparison of Vocational Training for Youth in Developing Countries: A Case Study of Four Training Models in Israel." *Comparative Education Review.* (21)1, 1977.

Carnoy, M., et. al. *Education, Work and Employment*. Paris: UNESCO, IIEP, 1980.

Castro, M. "Vocational Education and the Training of Industrial Labor in Brazil." *International Labor Review*. (118) 5, 1979.

Chin-Aleong, M. "Vocational Secondary Education in Trinidad and Tobago and Related Evaluation Results," in Lauglo and Lillis (eds.), *Vocationalising Education*. Oxford: Pergamon Press, 1988.

Chung, Y. "The Economic Returns to Vocational and Technical Education in A Fast-Growing Economy: A Case Study of Hong Kong." Doctoral Dissertation: Stanford University, 1987.

Cohen, S. *Malaysia: A Case for In-service Industrial Training*. Washington, D.C.: World Bank, 1983.

Cumming, C., et. al. " Curriculum Costs: Vocational Subjects," in Lauglo and Lillis (eds.), *Vocationalising Education*. Oxford: Pergamon Press, 1988.

Cumming, C., et. al. *Practical Subjects in Kenyan Academic Secondary Schools*. Stockholm: SIDA Education Division Document No. 22, 1985.

Farley, J. *Academic Women and Employment Discrimination: A Critical Annotated Bibliography*. Ithaca, New York: New York State School of Industrial and Labor Relations, 1982.

Figueroa, M. "Methodological Explorations on Schooling and the Reproduction of the Social Division of Labor: A Case Study of Mexico City." Doctoral Dissertation, Stanford University, 1986.

Foster, P. "The Vocational School Fallacy in Development Planning," in Anderson, C. and M. Bowman (eds.), *Education and Economic Development*. Chicago: Aldine, 1966.

Fuller, W. "Education, Training and Worker Productivity: Study of Skilled Workers in Two Firms in South India." Ph.D. Thesis: Stanford University, 1970.

Fuller, W. "More Evidence Supporting the Demise of Pre-employment Vocational Trade Training: A Case Study of A Factory in India." *Comparative Education Review*. (20)1, 1976.

Gallart, M. "The Secondarization of Secondary Education in Argentina and the Vocationalization of Secondary Education in Brazil," in Lauglo and Lillis (eds.) *Vocationalizing Education*, 1988.

Godfrey, M. "Education, Training and Productivity: A Kenyan Case Study." *Comparative Education Review*. (21)1, 1977.

Gustafsson, I. "Work as Education - Perspectives on the Role of Work in Current Educational Reform in Zimbabwe," in Lauglo and Lillis (eds.), *Vocationalising Education*. Oxford: Pergamon Press, 1988.

ILO *1987 Statistical Yearbook*, 1987.

ILO *1986 Statistical Yearbook*, 1986.

Lauglo, J. and A. Narman. "Diversified Secondary Education in Kenya: The Status of Practical Subjects and Their Use After School," in Lauglo and Lillis (eds.), *Vocationalising Education*. Oxford: Pergamon Press, 1988.

Levine, V. "Evaluating Vocational Training Alternatives Using Single Period Earnings Data: A Technical Note." *Comparative Education Review.* (23)1, 1979.

Little, A. *The Coordination of Education Policy and Planning and Employment Policy and Planning,* Vols. I and II, Paris: UNESCO, 1984.

Meyer, R. *An Economic Analysis of High School Vocational Education - IV. The Labor Market Effects of Vocational Education.* Washington, D.C.: The Urban Institute, 1981.

Min, W. and M. Tsang. *Vocational Education and Productivity: A Case Study of the Beijing General Auto Industry Company.* Stanford University, School of Education, 1987 (mimeo).

Noah, H. and M. Eckstein. " Business and Industry Involvement with Education in Britain, France and Germany," in Lauglo, J. and K. Lillis (eds.), *Vocationalising Education.* Oxford: Pergamon Press, 1988.

Puryear, J. "Vocational Training and Earnings in Colombia: Does a SENA Effect Exist?" *Comparative Education Review* (23)2, 1979.

Sanyal, B., et. al. *Higher Education and Labor Market in Zambia: Expectations and Performance.* Paris: UNESCO, IIEP, 1976.

Schiefelbein, E. and J. Farrell. *Eight Years Of Their Lives: Through Schooling to Labor Market in Chile.* Ottawa: IDRC, 1982.

Sewell, W. and R. Hauser. *Education, Occupation and Earnings: Achievement in the Early Career.* New York: Academic Press, 1975.

Tibi, C. "Report on Costs of Vocational and Technical Education in Thailand." Paris: IIEP, 1986 (mimeo in French).

Toussig, M. K. "An Economic Analysis of Vocational Education in the New York City High Schools." *Journal of Human Resources.* (3)5, 1968.

Vocational and Academic Secondary Education: What the Bank Has Done

Adams, A. and A. Schwartz. *Vocational Education and Economic Environments: Conflicts on Convergence,* PPR Working Paper No. 70, Washington, D.C.: World Bank, 1988.

Barker, H. *General Operational Review - Manpower and Training Issues in Sector Work.* PHREE Background Paper No. 88/02R, Washington, D.C.: World Bank, 1988.

Barker, H. *Guidelines for the Identification of Manpower and Training Issues in Non-Education Sector Work.* PHREE Background Paper No. 88/03, Washington, D.C.: World Bank, 1988.

Blomqvist, A. *Higher Education and the Markets for Educated Labour in LDCs: Theoretical Approaches and Implications.* EDT Discussion Paper No. 54, Washington, D.C.: World Bank, 1987.

Demsky, T. *Review of World Bank Investments in Vocational Education and Training for Commerce.* PHREE Background Paper No. 89/22, Washington, D.C.: World Bank, 1989.

Dougherty, C. *The Cost-Effectiveness of National Training Systems in Developing Countries.* PPR Working Paper No. 171, Washington, D.C.: World Bank, 1989.

Grootaert, C. *Côte d'Ivoire's Vocational and Technical Education.* PPR Working Paper No. 19, Washington, D.C.: World Bank, 1988.

Haddad, W. *Diversified Secondary Curriculum Projects: A Review of World Bank Experience, 1963-1979.* EDT Discussion Paper No. 57, Washington, D.C.: World Bank, 1987.

Haddad, W., G. Stevenson and A. Adams. *Youth Unemployment in the EMENA Region: An Issues Paper.* EDT Discussion Paper No. 76, Washington, D.C.: World Bank, 1987.

Heyneman, S. "Curricular Economics in Secondary Education: An Emerging Crisis in Developing Countries." *Prospects.* (17)1, 1987.

Hinchliffe, K. "Cost Structures of Secondary Schooling in Tanzania and Colombia." World Bank, 1983 (mimeo).

Inoue, K. *The Education and Training of Industrial Manpower in Japan.* World Bank Staff Working Paper No. 729, Washington, D.C.: World Bank, 1985.

Komenan, A. *Education, Experience, et Salaires en Côte d'Ivoire.* EDT Discussion Paper No. 99, Washington, D.C.: World Bank, 1987.

Lee, C. *Financing Technical Education in LDCs: Economic Implications from a Survey of Training Modes in the Republic of Korea.* EDT Discussion Paper No. 6, Washington, D.C.: World Bank, 1985.

Lee, K. *Human Resources Planning in the Republic of Korea: Improving Technical Education and Vocational Training.* World Bank Staff Working Paper No. 554, Washington, D.C.: World Bank, 1983.

Metcalf, D. *The Economics of Vocational Training: Past Evidence and Future Considerations.* World Bank Staff Working Paper No. 713, Washington, D.C.: World Bank, 1985.

Middleton, J. *Changing Patterns in Vocational Education.* PPR Working Paper No. 26, Washington, D.C.: World Bank, 1988.

Middleton, J. and T. Demsky. *World Bank Investments in Vocational Education and Training.* PPR Working Paper No. 24, Washington, D.C.: World Bank, 1988.

Mingat, A. "Measuring the Economic Efficiency of Project-related Training: Some Evidence From Agricultural Projects," 1984. (mimeo)

Moock, P. and R. Bellew. *Vocational and Technical Education in Peru.* PPR Working Paper No. 87, Washington, D.C.: World Bank, 1988.

Noah, H. and J. Middleton. *China's Vocational and Technical Training.* PPR Working Paper No. 18, Washington, D.C.: World Bank, 1988.

Paul, S. *Training for Public Administration and Management in Developing Countries: A Review.* World Bank Staff Working Paper No. 584, Washington, D.C.: World Bank, 1983.

Picciotto, R. *Chile Vocational Training Project — A Cost-Benefit Calculation.* Washington, D.C., 1965 (mimeo).

Psacharopoulos, G. and W. Loxley. *Diversified Secondary Education and Development: Evidence from Colombia and Tanzania.* Baltimore: Johns Hopkins University Press, 1985.

Psacharopoulos, G. and A. Zabalza. *The Destination and Early Career Performance of Secondary School Graduates in Colombia: Findings from the 1978 Cohort.* World Bank Staff Working Paper No. 653, Washington, D.C.: World Bank, May 1984.

Psacharopoulos, G. *To Vocationalize or Not to Vocationalize? That is the Curriculum Question.* EDT Discussion Paper No. 31, Washington, D.C.: World Bank, 1986.

Psacharopoulos, G. *Curriculum Diversification, Cognitive Achievement and Economic Performance: Evidence from Colombia and Tanzania.* EDT Discussion Paper No. 80, Washington, D.C.: World Bank, 1987.

Psacharopoulos, G. "Curriculum Diversification in Colombia and Tanzania: An Evaluation." *Comparative Education Review.* 1985.

Psacharopoulos, G. "Economics of Higher Education in Developing Countries." *Comparative Education* (26)2, 1982.

Schwartz, A. *The Dual Vocational Training System in the Federal Republic of Germany.* EDT Discussion Paper No. 36, Washington, D.C.: World Bank, 1986.

Stevenson, G. "Linkages Between the Macroeconomic Environment and Vocational Education: A Cost Study of the Republic of Korea." (forthcoming)

Velez, E. and G. Psacharopoulos. *The External Efficiency of Diversified Secondary Schools in Colombia.* EDT Discussion Paper No. 59, Washington, D.C.: World Bank, 1987.

World Bank, EMENA Education Division. *Regional Review of Alternative Modes of Vocational Training and Technical Education.* EDT Discussion Paper No. 41, Washington, D.C.: World Bank, 1986.

Ziderman, A. *Social Rates of Return to Manpower Training Programs: The Policy Context.* PHREE Background Paper No. 88/04, Washington, D.C.: World Bank, 1988.

Ziderman, A. "Training Alternatives for Youth: Results from Longitudinal Data." *Comparative Education Review* 33(2), 1989.

Ziderman, A. *Israel's Vocational Training.* PPR Working Paper No. 25, Washington, D.C.: World Bank, 1988.

Zymelman, M. *The Economic Evaluation of Vocational Training Programs.* Occasional Paper No. 21, Washington, D.C.: World Bank, 1976.

The Quality and Efficiency of Education: General

Carnoy, M. *Family Background, School Inputs and Students' Performance in School: The Case of Puerto Rico.* Stanford University, (mimeo) 1971.

Coleman, J., et. al. *High School Achievement: Public, Catholic and Private Schools Compared.* New York: Basic Books, 1982.

Coleman, J., et. al. *Equality of Educational Opportunity.* Washington, D.C.: Department of Health, Education, and Welfare, 1966.

Fuller, W. and A. Chantavanich. *A Study of Primary Schooling in Thailand: Factors Affecting Scholastic Achievement of the Primary School Pupils.* Bangkok: Office of the National Education Commission, 1976.

Haron, I. "Social Class and Educational Achievement in Plural Society: Peninsular Malaysia." Doctoral Dissertation: University of Chicago, 1977.

Levin, H. "Educational Production Theory and Teacher Inputs," in Bidwell, C. and D. Windham (eds.), *The Analysis of Educational Productivity: Issues in Macro Analysis.* Cambridge, MA.: Ballinger Publishing, 1980.

Loxley, N. *Quality of Schooling in the Kalahari.* Paper presented at the Meeting of the Comparative and International Education Society, Houston, Texas, 1984.

Moock, P. and R. Horn. "Overview of the World Bank's Research in Education." *Canadian and International Education.* (12), 1983.

Schiefelbein, E. and J. Farrell. *Factors Influencing Academic Performance Among Chilean Primary Students.* Santiago: Centro de Investigaciones y Desarrollo de la Educacion, 1973.

Sembiring, R. and I. Livingstone. *National Assessment of Quality of Indonesian Education.* Jakarta: Ministry of Education and Culture, 1981.

Solmon, L. "Quality of Education and Economic Growth." *Economics of Education Review*, 4(4), 1985.

Summers, A. and B. Wolfe. "Do Schools Make a Difference?" *American Economic Review.* (67)4, 1977.

Warren, J., et. al. "Differential Cost of Curricula in Illinois Public Junior Colleges: Some Implications for the Future." *Research in Higher Education.* (4), 1987.

The Quality and Efficiency of Education: What the Bank Has Done

Alexander, L. and J. Simmons. "The Determinants of School Achievement in Developing Countries: A Review of the Research." *Economic Development and Cultural Change* (2), 1978.

Armitage, Jane, et. al. *School Quality and Achievement in Rural Brazil.* EDT Discussion Paper No. 25, Washington, D.C.: World Bank, 1986.

Arriagada, A. M. "Determinants of Sixth Grade Student Achievement in Colombia," July 1981. (mimeo).

Arriagada, A. M. "Determinants of Sixth Grade Student Achievement in Peru," January 1983. (mimeo)

Behrman, J. and N. Birdsall. *The Implicit Equity-Productivity Takeoff in the Distribution of Public School Resources in Brazil.* Country Policy Paper, Washington, D.C.: World Bank, 1983.

Carnoy, M., R. Sack and H. Thias. *Determinants and Effects of School Performance: Secondary Education in Tunisia.* Washington, D.C.: World Bank, 1977.

Cochrane, S. and D. Jamison. *Educational Attainment and Achievement in Rural Thailand,* September 1982.

Cochrane, S., K. Mehra and I. Taha Osheba. *The Educational Participation of Egyptian Children.* EDT Discussion Paper No. 45, Washington, D.C.: World Bank, 1986.

Cochrane, S. and D. Jamison. "Educational Attainment and Achievement in Rural Thailand," in A. Summers (ed.). *New Directions for Testing and Measurement: Productivity Assessment in Education.* San Francisco: Jossey-Bass, 1982.

Cohn, E. and R. Rossmiller. *Research on Effective Schools: Implications for Less-Developed Countries.* EDT Discussion Paper No. 52, Washington, D.C.: World Bank, 1987.

Dutcher, N. *Use of First and Second Languages in Primary Education: Selected Case Studies.* World Bank Staff Working Paper No. 504, Washington, D.C.: World Bank, 1982.

Fuller, B. "Is Primary School Quality Eroding in the World?" *Comparative Education Review* (30)4, 1980.

Fuller, B. and M. Lockheed. *Policy Choice and School Efficiency in Mexico.* EDT Discussion Paper No. 78, Washington, D.C.: World Bank, 1987.

Fuller, B. "What School Factors Raise Achievement in the Third World?" *Review of Educational Research* (57)3, 1987.

Fuller, B. *Raising School Quality in Developing Countries: What Investments Boost Learning?* Washington, D.C.: World Bank, 1985.

Haddad, W. *Educational Effects of Class Size.* World Bank Staff Working Paper No. 280, Washington, D.C.: World Bank, 1978.

Haddad, W. *Teacher Training: A Review of World Bank Experience.* EDT Discussion Paper No. 21, Washington, D.C.: World Bank, 1986.

Haddad, W. *Educational and Economic Effects of Promotion and Repetition Practices.* World Bank Staff Working Paper No. 319, Washington, D.C.: World Bank, 1978.

Haddad, W. and G. Za'rour. *Role and Educational Effects of Practical Activities in Science Education.* EDT Discussion Paper No. 51, Washington, D.C.: World Bank, 1986.

Hartley, M. and E. Swanson. *Retention of Basic Skills Among Dropouts from Egyptian Primary Schools.* EDT Discussion Paper No. 40, Washington, D.C.: World Bank, 1986.

Heyneman, S. and W. Loxley. "The Effect of Primary School Quality on Academic Achievement Across Twenty-Nine High and Low Income Countries." *The American Journal of Sociology.* May 1983.

Heyneman, S. and W. Loxley. "Influences of Academic Achievement Across High and Low Income Countries: A Re-analysis of IEA Data." *Sociology of Education.* January 1982.

Heyneman, S. "Why Impoverished Children Do Well in Ugandan Schools." *Comparative Education.* (15), 1979.

Heyneman, S., J. Farrell and M. Sepulveda-Stuardo. *Textbooks and Achievement: What We Know.* World Bank Staff Working Paper No. 298, October 1978.

Heyneman, S. "Relationships Between the Primary School Community and Academic Achievement in Uganda." *The Journal of Developing Areas.* January 1977.

Heyneman, S. "Differences Between Developed and Developing Countries: Comment on Simmon and Alexander's "Determinants of School Achievement"." *Economic Development and Cultural Change.* January 1980.

Heyneman, S. and D. Jamison. "Student Learning in Uganda: Textbook Availability and Other Factors." *Comparative Education Review.* June 1980.

Horn, R. and Arriagada, A. M. *The Educational Attainment of the World's Population: Three Decades of Progress.* EDT Discussion Paper No. 37, Washington, D.C.: World Bank, September 1986.

Husen, T., et. al. *Teacher Training and Student Achievement in Less Developed Countries.* World Bank Staff Working Paper No. 310, Washington, D.C.: World Bank, 1978.

Jamison, D. "Improving Elementary Mathematics Education in Nicaragua: An Experimental Study of the Impact of Textbooks and Radio on Achievement." *Journal of Educational Psychology.* 1981.

Jamison, D. and M. Lockheed. "Participation in Schooling: Determinants and Learning Outcomes in Nepal." *Economic Development and Cultural Change.* 35(2), 1986.

Jimenez, E. and J. Tan. *Decentralization and Private Education: The Case of Pakistan.* EDT Discussion Paper No. 67, Washington, D.C.: World Bank, 1987.

Jimenez, E., M. Lockheed and N. Wattanawaha. *The Relative Effectiveness of Private and Public Schools in Enhancing Achievement: The Case of Thailand.* EDT Discussion Paper No. 97, Washington, D.C.: World Bank, 1987.

Lee, Valerie and M. Lockheed. "The Effects of Single-Sex Schools on Student Achievement and Attitudes in Nigeria." *Comparative Education Review.* (forthcoming)

Lockheed, M., B. Fuller and R. Nyirongo. *Family Background and Student Achievement.* PPR Working Paper No. 27, Washington, D.C.: World Bank, 1988.

Lockheed, M. *School and Classroom Effects on Student Learning Gain: The Case of Thailand.* EDT Discussion Paper No. 98, Washington, D.C.: World Bank, 1987.

Lockheed, M. and A. Komenan. *School Effects on Student Achievement in Nigeria and Swaziland.* PPR Working Paper 71, Washington, D.C.: World Bank, 1988.

Lockheed, M., S. Vail and B. Fuller. *How Textbooks Affect Achievement.* EDT Discussion Paper No. 53, Washington, D.C.: World Bank, 1987.

Lockheed, M. and E. Hanushek. *Improving the Efficiency of Education in Developing Countries: Review of the Evidence.* EDT Discussion Paper No. 77, Washington, D.C.: World Bank, 1987.

Lockheed, M. and K. Gorman. "Sociocultural Factors Affecting Science Learning and Attitude," in A. Champagne and L. Hornig (eds) *Students and Science Learning.* Washington: American Association for the Advancement of Science, 1987.

Lockheed, M. and A. Komenan. *School Effects on Student Achievement in Nigeria and Swaziland.* PPR Working Paper Series No. 71, Washington, D.C.: World Bank, 1988.

Lockheed, M. "How Textbooks Affect Achievement in Developing Countries: Evidence from Thailand." *Educational Evaluation and Policy Analysis.* 84(4), 1986.

Lockheed, M., et. al. Family Effects on Student Achievement in Thailand and Malawi. Washington, D.C.: World Bank, 1988 (mimeo).

Moock, P. and J. Leslie. "Childhood Malnutrition and Schooling in the Terai Region of Nepal." *Journal of Development Economics.* (20), 1986.

Pinera, S. and M. Selowsky. *The Economic Cost of the "Internal" Brain Drain: Its Magnitude in Developing Countries*, 1976.

Psacharopoulos, G. *School Participation, Grade Attainment and Literacy in Brazil: A 1980 Census Analysis.* EDT Discussion Paper No. 86, Washington, D.C.: World Bank, 1987.

Psacharopoulos, G. *Curriculum Diversification, Cognitive Achievement and Economic Performance: Evidence from Colombia and Tanzania.* EDT Discussion Paper No. 80, Washington, D.C.: World Bank, 1987.

Psacharopoulos, G. "Public Versus Private Schools in Developing Countries: Evidence from Colombia and Tanzania." *International Journal of Economic Development.* 1987.

Psacharopoulos, G. "Curriculum Diversification in Colombia and Tanzania: An Evaluation." *Comparative Education Review.* 1985.

Schiefelbein, E., J. Farrell and M. Sepulveda-Stuardo. *Influence of School Resources in Chile: Their Effect on Educational Achievement and Occupational Attainment.* World Bank Staff Working Paper No. 530, Washington, D.C.: World Bank, 1983.

Simmons, J. *How Effective is Schooling in Promoting Learning?: A Review of the Research.* Washington, D.C.: World Bank, 1975.

Smilansky, M. *Priorities in Education: Pre-school: Evidence and Conclusions.* World Bank Staff Working Paper No. 323, Washington, D.C.: World Bank, 1979.

Stromquist, N. *School-Related Determinants of Female Primary School Participation and Achievement in Developing Countries: An Annotated Bibliography.* EDT Discussion Paper No. 83, Washington, D.C.: World Bank, 1987.

Thias, H. and M. Carnoy. *Cost-Benefit Analysis in Education: A Case-Study of Kenya.* Baltimore: Johns Hopkins Press, 1972.

Verspoor, A. *Textbooks as Instruments for the Improvement of the Quality of Education.* EDT Discussion Paper No. 50, Washington, D.C.: World Bank, 1986.

Verspoor, A. *Pathways to Change: Improving the Quality of Education in Developing Countries.* World Bank Discussion Paper No. 53, kWashington, D.C.: World Bank, 1989.

Verspoor, A. and J. Leno. *Improving Teaching: A Key to Successful Educational Change.* EDT Discussion Paper No. 50, Washington, D.C.: World Bank, 1986.

Windham, D. *Internal Efficiency and the African School.* EDT Discussion Paper No. 47, Washington, D.C.: World Bank, 1986.

Zuzovsky, R. "Home and School Contributions to Science Achievement in Israel." Washington, D.C.: World Bank, PHREE, 1987, (mimeo).

Technology in Education: General

Anzalone, S. *Project Bridges: Hardware for Primary Education in Developing Countries: A Review of the Literature.* Harvard University, 1987.

Asian Development Bank. *Distance Education, Vols. I and II,* 1986.

Becker, H. *The Impact of Computer Use on Children's Learning.* Baltimore: Johns Hopkins University Press, 1987.

Block, C. "Interactive Radio and Educational Development: An Overview." *Developing Communications Report.* (49), 1985.

Carnoy, M., et. al. *Education and Computers: Visions and Realities in the Mid-1980s.* Stanford: Stanford University, 1986.

Carnoy, M. and L. Loop. *Computers and Education: Which Role for International Research?* Paris: UNESCO, 1986.

Carnoy, M. "The Economic Costs and Returns to Educational Television," in Arnove, R. F. (ed.), *Educational Television: A Policy Critique and Guide for Developing Countries.* New York: Praeger, 1976.

Clearinghouse on Development Communication. "Project Profiles," Washington, D.C.: *Clearinghouse on Development Communications,* 1982.

Freeman, C. *Computer Classroom Ethnography: Crochu Primary School, Grenada.* McLean, Virginia: Institute for International Research, Learning Technologies Project, 1987.

Friend, J. and S. Kozlow. *Evaluation of Second Grade Instructional Materials Produced by the Radio-assisted Community Basic Education Project.* Washington, D.C.: Inter-American Research Associates, 1985.

Jamison, D. and E. McAnany (eds.). *Radio for Education and Development.* Beverly Hills: Sage, 1978.

Kaye, A. "The Ivory Coast Educational Television Project," in Arnove, R. (ed.), Educational Television, 1976.

Kulik, J., C. Kulik and R. Bangert-Drowns. "Effectiveness of Computer Based Education in Elementary Schools." *Journal of Computers in Human Behaviour* 1:59-74, 1985.

Levin, H. M., et. al. *Improving Productivity Through Education and Technology.* Stanford: CERAS, 1984.

Mayo, J., et. al. *Educational Reform With Television: The El Salvador Experience.* Stanford: Stanford University, 1976.

Ministry of Education, Ethiopia. *Evaluation of Primary School Radio Programs.* Addis Ababa, 1987.

Neurath, P. *Radio Farm Forums in India.* New Delhi: Government of India Press, 1960.

Oxford R., et. al. *Final Report: Evaluation of the Kenya Radio Language Arts Project, Vol. I: Narrative Results.* Washington, D.C.: Academy for Educational Development, 1986.

Papagianis, G. *Information Technology and Education.* Ottawa: International Development Research Centre, 1987.

Roblyer, M., W. Castine and F. King. "The Effectiveness of Computers in Instruction: A Review and Synthesis of Recent Research Findings," 1987 (Submitted for Publication).

Schramm, W., et. al. *Bold Experiment: The Story of Educational Television in American Samoa.* Stanford, CA: Stanford University, 1981.

Schramm, W. (ed.). *New Educational Media in Action: Case Studies for Planners.* Paris: UNESCO, IIEP, 1967.

Shukla, P. *Satellite Instructional TV Experiment in India.* As cited in Anzalone, 1987.

Suppe, P., B. Searle, et. al. *The Radio Mathematics Project, Nicaragua.* Stanford, CA: Stanford University Press, 1978.

UNESCO. *New Educational Media in Action: Case Studies for Planners, Vols. I and II.* Paris: UNESCO, IIEP, 1976.

UNESCO. *The Economics of New Educational Media: Cost and Effectiveness, Vols. I and II.* Paris, 1984, Media Education. Paris, 1980.

Walker, H. *Evaluacion Cualitiva del Programa de Radioeducacion Comunitaria (RADECO) de la Republica Dominicana.* Washington, D.C.: USAID, 1986.

Williams, K. "Computers in Trinidad and Tobago: A Survey of Access and Attitudes Towards the Technology in Secondary Schools." Doctoral Dissertation. Cambridge, Massachusetts: Harvard University.

Technology in Education: What the Bank Has Done

Anzalone, S. "Educational Technology and the Improvement of General Education in Developing Countries." Washington, D.C.: World Bank, PHREE 1988 (mimeo).

Cassirer, H. "Radio in an African Context: A Description of Senegal's Pilot Project." in P. Spain, et al., *Radio for Education and Development.* Washington, D.C.: World Bank, 1977.

Feliciano, G., et. al. *The Educational Use of Mass Media.* World Bank Staff Working Paper No. 491, Washington, D.C.: World Bank, 1981.

Nettleton, G. "Uses and Costs of Educational Technology for Distance Education in Developing Countries: A Review of the Recent Literature." Washington, D.C.: World Bank (forthcoming)

Hawkridge, D. *General Operational Review of Distance Education.* EDT Discussion Paper No. 68, Washington, D.C.: World Bank, 1987.

Hall, B. and T. Dodds. "Voices for Development: The Tanzania National Radio Study Campaign" in P. Spain, et al., *Radio for Education and Development*. Washington, D.C.: World Bank, 1977.

Hudson, H. "Community Use of Radio in the Canadian North." in P. Spain, et al., *Radio for Education and Development*. Washington, D.C.: World Bank, 1977.

Jamison, D. *Radio Education and Student Repetition in Nicaragua*. World Bank Reprint Series No. 91, Washington, D.C.: World Bank, 1978.

Levin, H. "Educational Production Theory and Teacher Inputs" in C. Bidwell and D. Windham (eds.), *The Analysis of Productivity: Issues in Macro Analysis*. Cambridge, Mass.: Ballinger Publishing, 1980.

Perraton, H. (ed.). *Alternative Routes to Formal Education*. Baltimore: Johns Hopkins University, 1982.

Perraton, H. (ed.). *Distance Education: An Economic and Educational Assessment of its Potential for Africa*. EDT Discussion Paper No. 43, Washington, D.C.: World Bank, 1986.

Perrett, H. *Using Communication Support in Projects*. World Bank Staff Working Paper No. 551, Washington, D.C.: World Bank, 1982.

Spain, P. (ed.). *Radio for Education and Development: Case Studies*. World Bank Staff Working Paper No. 266, Washington, D.C.: World Bank, 1977.

Tiene, D. and S. Futagami. *Educational Media in Retrospect*. EDT Discussion Paper No. 58, Washington, D.C.: World Bank, 1987.

White, R. "Mass Communications and the Popular Promotion Strategy of Rural Development in Honduras," in Spain, P. L., et. al., *Radio for Education and Development, Vol. II*. Washington, D.C.: World Bank, 1977.

Sector Management General

Figueroa, M. *Methodological Explorations on Schooling and the Reproduction of the Social Division of Labor: A Case Study of Mexico City*. Doctoral dissertation, Stanford University, 1986.

Goodlad, J. *A Place Called School*. New York: McGraw-Hill, 1984.

Kulakow, A. M., et. al. *Mobilizing Rural Community Resources for Support and Development of Local Learning Systems in Developing Countries*. Washington, D.C.: Academy for Educational Development, 1978.

Meyer, J. "The Charter: Conditions of Diffused Socialization in Schools," in Scott, R. (ed.), *Social Processes and Social Structures*. New York: Holt, Rinehart and Winston, 1970.

Morales, J. and A. Pinellsiles. *The Determinant Factor and the Costs of Bolivia*. Working Paper No. 4-77. La Paz: Universidad Catolica Boliviana, 1977.

Meyer, J., et. al. *Bureaucratization Without Centralization: Changes in the Organizational System of American Public Education, 1940-1980*. Palo Alto: CERAS, Stanford University, 1985.

National Commission on Excellence in Education. *A Nation At Risk.* Washington, D.C.: Government Printing Office, 1983.

Sembiring, R. and I. Livingstone. *National Assessment of Quality of Indonesian Education.* Ministry of Education and Culture, Jakarta, Indonesia, 1981.

Sector Management: What the Bank Has Done

Auerhan, J., et. al. *A Study of Institutional Development in Education and Training in Sub-Saharan African Countries.* EDT Discussion Paper No. , Washington, D. C.: World Bank, November 1985.

Craig, J. *Implementing Educational Policies in Sub-Saharan Africa, A Review of the Literature.* EDT Discussion Paper No. 79, Washington, D.C.: World Bank, May 1987.

Fullan, M. "Implementing Educational Change - What We Know." PHREE Background Paper No. 89/18, Washington, D.C.: World Bank, 1989.

Fuller, B. "What School Factors Raise Achievement in the Third World?" *Review of Educational Research* (57)3, 1987.

Fuller, B. and M. Lockheed. *Policy Choice and School Efficiency in Mexico: An Analysis of the Impact of National Policy Decisions on Student Achievement.* EDT Discussion Paper No. 78, Washington, D.C.: World Bank, May 1987.

Haddad, W., et. al. "A Conceptual Framework for Policy Analysis," 1987. (mimeo)

Heyneman, S. and W. Loxley. "The Effect of Primary School Quality on Academic Achievement Across 29 High- and Low-Income Countries." *American Journal of Sociology.* (88)6, 1983.

James, E. *The Political Economy of Private Education in Developing Countries.* EDT Discussion Paper No. 71, Washington, D. C.: World Bank, May 1987.

Jimenez, E. and J. Tan. *Decentralized and Private Education: The Case of Pakistan,* EDT Discussion Paper No. 61, Washington, D. C.: World Bank, 1988.

Jimenez, E., et. al. *The Relative Effectiveness of Private and Public Schools in Enhancing Achievement: The Case of Thailand.* EDT Discussion Paper No. 97, Washington, D. C.: World Bank, June 1987.

Middleton, J., James Terry and Deborah Bloch. *Building Educational Evaluation Capacity in Developing Countries.* PPR Working Paper No. 140. Washington, D.C.: World Bank, 1989.

Middleton, J., H. Woldemariam and C. Mayo-Brown. *Management in World Bank Education Projects: Analysis of Experience.* EDT Discussion Paper No. 42, Washington, D.C.: World Bank, 1986.

Middleton, J., D. Rondinelli and A. Verspoor. *Designing Management for Uncertainty and Innovation in Education Projects.* EDT Discussion Paper No. 75 , Washington, D. C.: World Bank, April 1987.

Noor, A. A General Operational Review: "Strengthening Educational Management: A Review of World Bank Assistance," 1985. (mimeo)

Somerset, H. *Case Study on Examinations Reform: The Kenya Experience, 1983.* EDT Discussion Paper No. 64, Washington, D. C.: World Bank, 1987.

Verspoor, A. *Project Management for Educational Change.* EDT Discussion Paper No. 12, Washington, D.C.: World Bank, 1985.

Verspoor, A. *Implementing Educational Change: The World Bank Experience.* EDT Discussion Paper No. 44, Washington, D.C.: World Bank, 1986.

Winkler, D. "Decentralization in Education. An Economic Perspective." PPR Working Paper No. 143, Washington, D.C.: World Bank, 1989.

Science Education: General

King, K. (ed.). *Science Education and Society: Perspectives from India and South East Asia.* Ottawa: International Development Research Centre, 1985.

Morris, R.W. (ed.). *Science and Technology Education and National Development.* Paris: UNESCO, 1983.

Raizen, S. *Increasing Educational Productivity Through Improving the Science Curriculum.* New Brunswick, NJ: Rutgers University, Center for Policy Research in Education, 1988.

Suppe, P., et al., *The Radio Mathematics Project: Nicaragua.* Stanford: Stanford University Press, 1978.

U.S. Congress, Office of Technology Assessment. *Special Report on Information Technology and Education.* Washington, D.C.: U.S. Government Printing Office, 1988.

Science Education: What the Bank Has Done

Haddad, W. and G. Za'rour. *Role and Educational Effects of Practical Activities in Science Education.* EDT Discussion Paper No. 51, Washington, D. C.: World Bank, 1986.

Higher Education and Technology Transfer: General

Asian Development Bank. *Distance Education: Volumes I and II.* Manila: Asian Development Bank, 1986.

Bianchi, P., M. Carnoy and M. Castells. *Economic Reform and Technology Transfer in China.* Stanford University: CERAS, 1988.

Carnoy, M. "High Technology and Education: An Economist's View." in *Society as Educator in an Age of Transition.* Chicago: National Society for the Study of Education, 1987.

Coleman, J.S., et al., *High School Achievement: Public, Catholic and Private Schools Compared.* New York: Basic Books, 1982.

Edquist, C. *Capitalism, Socialism and Technology: A Comparative Study of Cuba and Jamaica.* London: Zed, 1985.

Edquist, C. and S. Jacobsson. *Flexible Automation: The Global Diffusion of New Technologies in the Engineering Industry.* London: Basil Blackwell, 1988.

National Science Foundation. *Science and Engineering Education for the 1980s and Beyond.* Washington, D.C.: NSF, Department of Education, 1980.

Ritter, U. *Higher Education by the Year 2000.* New York, Campus Publications, 1985.

Rosenberg, N. *Inside the Black Box.* Cambridge: Cambridge University Press, 1982.

U. S. House of Representatives, Committee on Science and Technology (98th Session). *U.S. Science and Engineering Education and Manpower.* Washington, D.C.: U. S. Government Printing Office, 1983.

Useem, E. *Low Tech Education in a High Tech World.* New York: Free Press, 1986.

Higher Education and Technology Transfer: What the Bank Has Done

Bowman, M., B. Millot and E. Schiefelbein. *The Political Economy of Higher Education: Studies in Chile, France and Malaysia.* EDT Discussion Paper No. 30, Washington, D.C.: World Bank, 1986.

Hinchliffe, K. *Issues Related to Higher Education in Sub-Saharan Africa.* World Bank Staff Working Paper No. 729, Washington, D.C.: World Bank, 1985.

Perraton, H. *Alternative Routes to Formal Education: Distance Teaching for School Equivalency,* Baltimore: Johns Hopkins University Press, 1982.

Weiss, C. "Science and Technology and the World Bank," July 1983. (mimeo)

Za'rour, G. *Status of Universities in the Arab Countries of the Middle East and North Africa.* PPR Working Paper No. 62, Washington, D.C.: World Bank, 1988.

Educational Finance Reform: General

Armitage, J. and R. Sabot. "Efficiency and Equity Implications of Subsidies of Secondary Education in Kenya," in Newberry, D. and N. Stern (eds.), *Modern Tax Theories For Developing Countries.* New York: Oxford University Press, 1985.

Gustafsson, I. *Work as Education — Perspectives on the Role of Work in Current Educational Reform in Zimbabwe.* Oxford: Pergamon Press, 1988.

Eicher, J. C. *Educational Costing and Financing in Developing Countries.* Staff Working Paper No. 655, Washington, D.C.: World Bank, 1984.

Hansen, W. and B. Weisbrod. *Benefits, Costs and Finance of Public Higher Education.* Chicago: Markham Publishing Company, 1969.

Heller, P. and A. Cheasty. "Sectoral Adjustment in Government Expenditure in the 1970s: The Education Sector in Latin America." *World Development.* (12), 1984.

Kulakow, A., et al. *Mobilising Rural Community Resources for Support and Development of Local Learning Systems on Developoing Countries.* Washington, D.C.: Academy for Educational Development, 1978.

Levin, H. *New Schools for the Disadvantaged.* Stanford: CERAS, 1987.

Levin, H. "Education As A Public and Private Good." *Journal of Policy Analysis.* (6), 1987.

Meeth, L. R. *A Curricular and Financial Cost Analysis of the Independent Two Year College of America.* Washington, D.C.: National Council of Independent Junior Colleges, 1974.

Smock, A. *Women's Education in Developing Countries: Opportunities and Outcomes.* New York: Praeger, 1981.

Yao Yao, J. "The Redistribution of Earnings in the Ivory Coast: The Role of Higher Education Finance." Doctoral Dissertation, Stanford University, 1987.

Educational Finance Reform: What the Bank Has Done

Castenada, T. *Innovations in the Financing of Education: The Case of Chile.* EDT Discussion Paper No. 35, Washington, D.C.: World Bank, 1986.

Eicher, J. C. *Educational Costing and Financing in Developing Countries.* World Bank Staff Working Paper No. 655, Washington, D.C.: 1984.

Hinchliffe, K. *Federal Finance, Fiscal Imbalance and Educational Inequality.* EDT Discussion Paper No. 72, Washington, D.C.: World Bank, 1987.

Hultin, M. and J. P. Jallade. *Costing and Financing Education in LDCs: Current Issues.* World Bank Staff Working Paper No. 216, Washington, D.C.: World Bank, 1975.

Jallade, J. P. *Public Expenditures on Education and Income Distribution in Colombia.* Baltimore: Johns Hopkins University Press, 1974.

Jallade, J. P. *Student Loans in Developing Countries: An Evaluation of Colombian Performance.* World Bank Staff Working Paper No. 182, 1974.

Jallade, J. P. *Poverty Alleviation and Educational Lending: Present Practice and Future Prospects.* Washington, D.C.: World Bank, 1982.

Jallade, J. P. *Financing of Education: An Examination of Basic Issues.* World Bank Staff Working Paper No. 157, Washington, D.C.: World Bank, 1973.

Jimenez, E. *Pricing Policy in the Social Sectors: Cost Recovery for Education and Health in Developing Countries.* Baltimore: Johns Hopkins University Press, 1987.

Jimenez, E. "Structure of Educational Costs: Multiproduct Cost Funcations for Primary and Secondary Schools in Latin America." *Economics of Education Review.* 5, 1986.

Jimenez, E., M. Lockheed and N. Wattananwaha. "The Relative Efficiency of Private and Public Schools: The Case of Thailand. *The World Bank Economic Review.* (2)2, 1988.

Mingat, A. and J. P. Tan. "Expanding Education Through User Changes in LDCs: What Can Be Achieved?" *Economics of Education Review* 5(3), 1986.

Psacharopoulos, G., "Economics of Higher Education in Developing Countries." *Comparative Economic Review.* (26)2, 1982.

Psacharopoulos, G., *Economics of Education.* Oxford: Pergamon Press, 1987.

Psacharopoulos, G., "Curriculum Diversification, Cognitive Achievement and Economic Performance: Evidence from Colombia and Tanzania." in J. Lauglo and K. Lillis (eds.), *Vocationalising Education.* Oxford: Pergamon Press, 1988.

Psacharopoulos, G., J.P. Tan and E. Jimenez. *The Financing of Higher Education in Latin America: Issues and Lines of Action.* EDT Discussion Paper No. 32, Washington, D.C.: 1986.

Schiefelbein, E. *Education, Costs and Financing Policies in Latin America.* EDT Discussion Paper No. 60, Washington, D.C.: World Bank, 1985.

Tan, J. P., et. al. *User Charges for Education: The Ability and Willingness to Pay in Malawi.* World Bank Staff Working Paper No. 661, Washington, D.C.: World Bank, 1984.

Wolff, L. *Controlling the Cost of Education in Eastern Africa.* World Bank Staff Working Paper No. 702, Washington, D.C.: World Bank, 1984.

Woodhall, M. *Student Loans as a Means of Financing Higher Education: Lessons from International Experience.* World Bank Staff Working Paper No. 599, Washington, D.C.: World Bank, 1983.

World Bank. *Financing Education in Developing Countries: An Exploration of Policy Options.* Washington, D.C.: World Bank, 1986.

Distributors of World Bank Publications

ARGENTINA
Carlos Hirsch, SRL
Galeria Guemes
Florida 165, 4th Floor-Ofc. 453/465
1333 Buenos Aires

AUSTRALIA, PAPUA NEW GUINEA, FIJI, SOLOMON ISLANDS, VANUATU, AND WESTERN SAMOA
D.A. Books & Journals
648 Whitehorse Road
Mitcham 3132
Victoria

AUSTRIA
Gerold and Co.
Graben 31
A-1011 Wien

BAHRAIN
Bahrain Research and Consultancy Associates Ltd.
P.O. Box 22103
Manama Town 317

BANGLADESH
Micro Industries Development Assistance Society (MIDAS)
House 5, Road 16
Dhanmondi R/Area
Dhaka 1209

Branch offices:
156, Nur Ahmed Sarak
Chittagong 4000

76, K.D.A. Avenue
Kulna

BELGIUM
Publications des Nations Unies
Av. du Roi 202
1060 Brussels

BRAZIL
Publicacoes Tecnicas Internacionais Ltda.
Rua Peixoto Gomide, 209
01409 Sao Paulo, SP

CANADA
Le Diffuseur
C.P. 85, 1501B rue Ampère
Boucherville, Québec
J4B 5E6

CHINA
China Financial & Economic Publishing House
8, Da Fo Si Dong Jie
Beijing

COLOMBIA
Enlace Ltda.
Apartado Aereo 34270
Bogota D.E.

COTE D'IVOIRE
Centre d'Edition et de Diffusion Africaines (CEDA)
04 B.P. 541
Abidjan 04 Plateau

CYPRUS
MEMRB Information Services
P.O. Box 2098
Nicosia

DENMARK
SamfundsLitteratur
Rosenoerns Allé 11
DK-1970 Frederiksberg C

DOMINICAN REPUBLIC
Editora Taller, C. por A.
Restauración e Isabel la Católica 309
Apartado Postal 2190
Santo Domingo

EL SALVADOR
Fusades
Avenida Manuel Enrique Araujo #3530
Edificio SISA, 1er. Piso
San Salvador

EGYPT, ARAB REPUBLIC OF
Al Ahram
Al Galaa Street
Cairo

The Middle East Observer
8 Chawarbi Street
Cairo

FINLAND
Akateeminen Kirjakauppa
P.O. Box 128
SF-00101
Helsinki 10

FRANCE
World Bank Publications
66, avenue d'Iéna
75116 Paris

GERMANY, FEDERAL REPUBLIC OF
UNO-Verlag
Poppelsdorfer Allee 55
D-5300 Bonn 1

GREECE
KEME
24, Ippodamou Street Platia Plastiras
Athens-11635

GUATEMALA
Librerias Piedra Santa
5a. Calle 7-55
Zona 1
Guatemala City

HONG KONG, MACAO
Asia 2000 Ltd.
Mongkok Post Office
Bute Street No. 37
Mongkok, Kowloon
Hong Kong

HUNGARY
Kultura
P.O. Box 149
1389 Budapest 62

INDIA
Allied Publishers Private Ltd.
751 Mount Road
Madras - 600 002

Branch offices:
15 J.N. Heredia Marg
Ballard Estate
Bombay - 400 038

13/14 Asaf Ali Road
New Delhi - 110 002

17 Chittaranjan Avenue
Calcutta - 700 072

Jayadeva Hostel Building
5th Main Road Gandhinagar
Bangalore - 560 009

3-5-1129 Kachiguda Cross Road
Hyderabad - 500 027

Prarthana Flats, 2nd Floor
Near Thakore Baug, Navrangpura
Ahmedabad - 380 009

Patiala House
16-A Ashok Marg
Lucknow - 226 001

INDONESIA
Pt. Indira Limited
Jl. Sam Ratulangi 37
P.O. Box 181
Jakarta Pusat

ITALY
Licosa Commissionaria Sansoni SPA
Via Benedetto Fortini, 120/10
Casella Postale 552
50125 Florence

JAPAN
Eastern Book Service
37-3, Hongo 3-Chome, Bunkyo-ku 113
Tokyo

KENYA
Africa Book Service (E.A.) Ltd.
P.O. Box 45245
Nairobi

KOREA, REPUBLIC OF
Pan Korea Book Corporation
P.O. Box 101, Kwangwhamun
Seoul

KUWAIT
MEMRB Information Services
P.O. Box 5465

MALAYSIA
University of Malaya Cooperative Bookshop, Limited
P.O. Box 1127, Jalan Pantai Baru
Kuala Lumpur

MEXICO
INFOTEC
Apartado Postal 22-860
14060 Tlalpan, Mexico D.F.

MOROCCO
Société d'Etudes Marketing Marocaine
12 rue Mozart, Bd. d'Anfa
Casablanca

NETHERLANDS
InOr-Publikaties b.v.
P.O. Box 14
7240 BA Lochem

NEW ZEALAND
Hills Library and Information Service
Private Bag
New Market
Auckland

NIGERIA
University Press Limited
Three Crowns Building Jericho
Private Mail Bag 5095
Ibadan

NORWAY
Narvesen Information Center
Book Department
P.O. Box 6125 Etterstad
N-0602 Oslo 6

OMAN
MEMRB Information Services
P.O. Box 1613, Seeb Airport
Muscat

PAKISTAN
Mirza Book Agency
65, Shahrah-e-Quaid-e-Azam
P.O. Box No. 729
Lahore 3

PERU
Editorial Desarrollo SA
Apartado 3824
Lima

PHILIPPINES
National Book Store
701 Rizal Avenue
P.O. Box 1934
Metro Manila

POLAND
ORPAN
Palac Kultury i Nauki
00-901 Warszawa

PORTUGAL
Livraria Portugal
Rua Do Carmo 70-74
1200 Lisbon

SAUDI ARABIA, QATAR
Jarir Book Store
P.O. Box 3196
Riyadh 11471

MEMRB Information Services
Branch offices:
Al Alsa Street
Al Dahna Center
First Floor
P.O. Box 7188
Riyadh

Haji Abdullah Alireza Building
King Khaled Street
P.O. Box 3969
Damman

33, Mohammed Hassan Awad Street
P.O. Box 5978
Jeddah

SINGAPORE, TAIWAN, MYANMAR, BRUNEI
Information Publications Private, Ltd.
02-06 1st Fl., Pei-Fu Industrial Bldg.
24 New Industrial Road
Singapore 1953

SOUTH AFRICA, BOTSWANA
For single titles:
Oxford University Press Southern Africa
P.O. Box 1141
Cape Town 8000

For subscription orders:
International Subscription Service
P.O. Box 41095
Craighall
Johannesburg 2024

SPAIN
Mundi-Prensa Libros, S.A.
Castello 37
28001 Madrid

Librería Internacional AEDOS
Consell de Cent, 391
08009 Barcelona

SRI LANKA AND THE MALDIVES
Lake House Bookshop
P.O. Box 244
100, Sir Chittampalam A. Gardiner Mawatha
Colombo 2

SWEDEN
For single titles:
Fritzes Fackboksforetaget
Regeringsgatan 12, Box 16356
S-103 27 Stockholm

For subscription orders:
Wennergren-Williams AB
Box 30004
S-104 25 Stockholm

SWITZERLAND
For single titles:
Librairie Payot
6, rue Grenus
Case postale 381
CH 1211 Geneva 11

For subscription orders:
Librairie Payot
Service des Abonnements
Case postale 3312
CH 1002 Lausanne

TANZANIA
Oxford University Press
P.O. Box 5299
Dar es Salaam

THAILAND
Central Department Store
306 Silom Road
Bangkok

TRINIDAD & TOBAGO, ANTIGUA BARBUDA, BARBADOS, DOMINICA, GRENADA, GUYANA, JAMAICA, MONTSERRAT, ST. KITTS & NEVIS, ST. LUCIA, ST. VINCENT & GRENADINES
Systematics Studies Unit
#9 Watts Street
Curepe
Trinidad, West Indies

TURKEY
Haset Kitapevi, A.S.
Istiklal Caddesi No. 469
Beyoglu
Istanbul

UGANDA
Uganda Bookshop
P.O. Box 7145
Kampala

UNITED ARAB EMIRATES
MEMRB Gulf Co.
P.O. Box 6097
Sharjah

UNITED KINGDOM
Microinfo Ltd.
P.O. Box 3
Alton, Hampshire GU34 2PG
England

URUGUAY
Instituto Nacional del Libro
San Jose 1116
Montevideo

VENEZUELA
Libreria del Este
Aptdo. 60.337
Caracas 1060-A

YUGOSLAVIA
Jugoslovenska Knjiga
P.O. Box 36
Trg Republike
YU-11000 Belgrade